ADVANCE PRAISE FOR *MENDOZA THE JEW*

With *Mendoza the Jew*, Ronald Schechter has produced an exceptional work of history that combines the scholar's attention to historical accuracy and documentation with the story-teller's gift for making the past come alive. The graphic novel format, with illustrations by Liz Clarke, engages the reader by conveying the emotion and drama of Mendoza's story. The choice to include the author and his quest for answers in the narrative creates another layer of interest. The included documentation enriches and complicates the historical narrative, providing much food for thought and analysis. While any fan of history will enjoy this work, teachers and students alike will appreciate the opportunities for creative learning presented by *Mendoza the Jew*. It is destined to become a classroom classic.

VICTORIA THOMPSON, *Arizona State University*

Mendoza the Jew is an intriguing micro-study of a cultural theme that opens the door to larger issues. The combination of graphics and primary sources offers unique opportunities for students to practice the work of a historian and to see how historians interpret the material they uncover.

DEAN BELL, *Spertus Institute of Jewish Studies*

Mendoza the Jew forces the students to engage with primary source documents in a way that most secondary accounts do not—and cannot. This is a book that will make the students learn how to ply the craft of history, the aim to which almost all teachers of history aspire.

MARK RUFF, *St. Louis University*

National identity is uniquely explored in Schechter's retelling of Mendoza's life. Mendoza and the early boxing world foreshadow the crossroads of nationalism and masculinity which come into full bloom nearly one hundred years later.

MARYANNE RHETT, *Monmouth University*

Mendoza the Jew gives students the chance to really understand how secondary source information is constructed based on primary source information: it does this by having students act as historians.

ROBERT BRENNAN, *Cape Fear Community College*

MENDOZA THE JEW

BOXING, MANLINESS, AND NATIONALISM

A GRAPHIC HISTORY

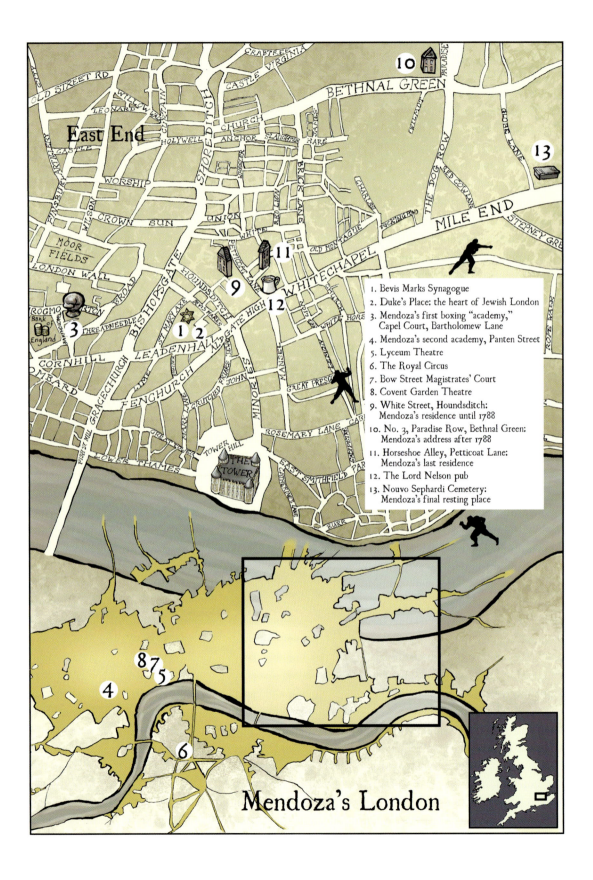

East End

BETHNAL GREEN

MILE END

WHITECHAPEL

1. Bevis Marks Synagogue
2. Duke's Place: the heart of Jewish London
3. Mendoza's first boxing "academy,"
   Capel Court, Bartholomew Lane
4. Mendoza's second academy, Panten Street
5. Lyceum Theatre
6. The Royal Circus
7. Bow Street Magistrates' Court
8. Covent Garden Theatre
9. White Street, Houndsditch:
   Mendoza's residence until 1788
10. No. 3, Paradise Row, Bethnal Green:
    Mendoza's address after 1788
11. Horseshoe Alley, Petticoat Lane:
    Mendoza's last residence
12. The Lord Nelson pub
13. Nouvo Sephardi Cemetery:
    Mendoza's final resting place

Mendoza's London

MENDOZA THE JEW

BOXING, MANLINESS, AND NATIONALISM
A GRAPHIC HISTORY

RONALD SCHECHTER

LIZ CLARKE

New York Oxford
OXFORD UNIVERSITY PRESS

Oxford University Press is a department of the University of Oxford.
It furthers the University's objective of excellence in research,
scholarship, and education by publishing worldwide.

Oxford   New York
Auckland   Cape Town   Dar es Salaam   Hong Kong   Karachi
Kuala Lumpur   Madrid   Melbourne   Mexico City   Nairobi
New Delhi   Shanghai   Taipei   Toronto

With offices in
Argentina   Austria   Brazil   Chile   Czech Republic   France   Greece
Guatemala   Hungary   Italy   Japan   Poland   Portugal   Singapore
South Korea   Switzerland   Thailand   Turkey   Ukraine   Vietnam

Copyright © 2014 by Oxford University Press

For titles covered by Section 112 of the US Higher Education
Opportunity Act, please visit www.oup.com/us/he for the latest
information about pricing and alternate formats.

Published by Oxford University Press
198 Madison Avenue, New York, NY 10016
www.oup.com

ISBN 978-0-19-933409-4

Printing number: 9 8 7 6 5 4 3 2 1

Printed in the United States of America
on acid-free paper

To my mother, Marilyn Schechter,
and to the memory of my father, David Schechter (1939–2011)

CONTENTS

MAPS AND FIGURES

MAPS

FIGURES

PREFACE

Perhaps you have heard this story before. A member of an ethnic minority grows up on the rough side of town. Prejudice and lack of financial resources limit his opportunities in life, but he soon discovers that he has athletic abilities, and that people are willing to pay to watch him perform. His sport offers him the chance to earn more money than he could have dreamed of and to socialize with the rich and famous. He becomes a star, a household name, the object of intense media attention, and a hero to members of his ethnic group, who see him as a symbol of their hope to escape poverty and degradation. He is also a symbol of his country, since his fellow citizens see his sport as embodying the nation and its values—strength, determination, courage—and many are willing to overlook the fact that he is, well, different. Yet he has many detractors, some of whom are motivated by envy or prejudice; they wait for him to slip up, and they are happy when it turns out that he is not a model of virtue. He lives lavishly, spends more quickly than he earns, and gets into trouble with the law. Eventually he doesn't even have the distinction of being criticized, as the fickle media turn their attention elsewhere and our former sports star descends into obscurity.

This is the story of many professional athletes in the twentieth and twenty-first centuries. Yet it is also the story of Daniel Mendoza, a British boxing champion who fought over 200 years ago. Born in the East End of London in 1765 to Jewish parents of limited means, Daniel grew up in a difficult environment. Faced with the prejudice of his non-Jewish neighbors, he responded to anti-Semitic taunts with his fists. Soon his reputation as a boxer spread, and he obtained opportunities to fight for prize money. By the end of the 1780s he had become a star. Thousands of spectators paid to watch his matches—and to bet on the outcome—and thousands more read about his bouts in the newspapers. He was one of the very first national sports heroes, both in the sense of being famous outside his city of origin and in the sense of symbolizing a sport that many regarded as particular to their "nation." Boxing fans often claimed that their sport was essentially British. Unlike the French, who reputedly settled their disputes by dueling with swords or pistols, the British had (in the words of boxing enthusiasts) a more "natural" and "manly" way of defending their honor: by using their fists. Paradoxically, an outsider, a Jew with a Hispanic name, came to epitomize a "British" sport. Many of his coreligionists became his pupils, and a generation of Jewish boxers, now largely forgotten, carried on the tradition that Mendoza started. Yet Mendoza was only human, and he succumbed to the temptations of sudden wealth and fame. He spent beyond his means and repeatedly found himself in legal trouble. Meanwhile his fair-weather friends disappeared and his adversaries gloated over his misfortunes.

Why should Mendoza's story matter to us today? To begin with, it sheds light on the origins of celebrity sports culture, which began in eighteenth-century Britain and has been with us for more than two centuries. It also reveals another legacy of the century that is normally viewed from a different angle: nationalism. Historians typically study nationalism in terms of learned treatises and political speeches, whereas eighteenth-century British boxing shows us how ideas and emotions regarding the "nation" permeated the practices of everyday life. Moreover, Mendoza's story reveals ambivalent attitudes of a society towards its minorities, who were allowed (sometimes grudgingly) to participate in national life by braving pain and injury in athletic contests but whose social mobility was limited and precarious. We might rightly ask, to what extent is our society different? Finally, Mendoza's story is relevant to our understanding of gender, or how ideas about what is "manly" or "effeminate" define a particular society's values and power relations. When supporters of boxing praised their sport as manly, or when a boxer questioned the "manliness" of his opponent's behavior, they implicitly relegated all "effeminate" people to the margins of society and deemed them unfit for respect. This was not an inevitable way of dividing up the world, though it is largely with us still.

Mendoza the Jew is divided into five parts, each with its own purpose.

Part I is a graphic history. It relates the narrative of Mendoza's life and career, with particular emphasis on the boxer's rivalry with Richard Humphries. It is the product of my collaboration with graphic artist Liz Clarke, who has taken the story and text I assembled from historical sources and infused it with beautiful images that evoke emotion and action. A work in its own right, the graphic history can be read on its own, but I hope you will not stop there.

Part II consists of primary sources—in other words, original sources from the period under consideration. These sources give you a deeper understanding of the story told in Part I. They will transport you directly into Mendoza's world. They will also enable you to question and critique the graphic history by comparing it to the sources on which it is based.

Reading them will give you the tools to engage in the same kind of historical analysis that professional historians engage in.

Part III provides you with the historical context to enrich your understanding of both the graphic history and the primary sources. It gives you information about the history of the Jews in eighteenth-century Britain, prejudice and tolerance in British society, the rise of spectator sports, the history of boxing in particular, and developments in the history of nationalism and gender.

Part IV is an account of the process by which Liz and I produced the book you are reading. It is meant to give you a still clearer sense of how the discipline of history works.

Part V consists of suggested writing assignments that enable you to "be your own historian" by interpreting the primary sources and critiquing the graphic history. It is written with the conviction that you truly understand how a work of history is produced only when you begin to make one for yourself.

Taken together, the five parts function as a lesson in historical methodology. When you are finished with this book, you will have not only a deeper understanding of the issues outlined in the previous paragraph (e.g., the history of celebrity sports culture, prejudice and tolerance, nationalism, and gender), but also a deeper understanding of how the discipline of history works.

ACKNOWLEDGMENTS

I owe a debt of gratitude to many people who have played a role in the making of this book. Liz Clarke has not only amazed me with her stunning art work, she has also helped me focus and clarify my ideas and saved me from more than one embarrassing error. Karlyn Hixson, the Oxford University Press representative for Virginia, Maryland, and Washington, DC, stimulated my interest in the graphic history form by introducing me to *Abina and the Important Men*, which inspired me to begin work on *Mendoza the Jew*. Charles Cavaliere, editor for world history textbooks at OUP, believed in this project from the beginning and has played a role in every phase of its development. He has carefully read every word, examined every image, and given unfailingly sage advice on everything from the fonts we have used to the cover design. The following reviewers took time out of their busy schedules to evaluate the proposal for this book: Abel A. Alves, Ball State University; David A. Bell, Princeton University; Dean Bell, Spertus Institute of Jewish Studies; Rafe Blaufarb, Florida State University; Robert Bond, San Diego Mesa College; Robert Brennan, Cape Fear Community College; David M. Kalivas, Middlesex Community College; John Moser, Ashland University; Mark Edward Ruff, Saint Louis University; Annemarie Sammartino, Oberlin College; Victoria E. Thompson, Arizona State University; Janet M. C. Walmsley, George Mason University; and Molly A. Warsh, University of Pittsburgh.

Once the text and artwork were submitted, Keith Faivre efficiently shepherded the book through its many stages of production. I was fortunate to have Mary Anne Shahidi as my eagle-eyed copyeditor and the talented Michele Laseau and Bonni Leon-Berman as the book's designers. At the College of William and Mary I had the good fortune to work with Kathleen DeLaurenti, an exceptional reference librarian who helped me find and organize visual materials from the eighteenth century, and Sagra Alvarado, an outstanding research assistant who made my work easier by transcribing often barely legible articles about Mendoza from the 17th and 18th Century Burney Collection Newspapers database. Computer wizard Pablo Yañez found the fonts that we used in the graphic history when quoting Mendoza's memoirs and an eighteenth-century newspaper. Friends and colleagues too numerous to name read selections of the book in progress and offered comments and encouragement. I have also been fortunate to have the support of my family. My spouse, Ute Schechter, cheerfully indulged my unexpected preoccupation with boxing, even to the point of watching boxing movies with me. My son, Arthur Schechter, took an early interest in this book and asked me on many occasions, "How's Mendoza?" My mother, Marilyn Schechter, took me to the Muhammad Ali Museum in my hometown of Louisville, Kentucky, and relayed the tantalizing (but as yet undocumented) story that my great-grandmother's cousin was Max Baer, a Jewish boxing champion from another time and place.

ABOUT THE AUTHOR

Ronald Schechter is Associate Professor of History at the College of William and Mary, where he has taught since 1997. He received his BA from the University of Michigan (1987), his MA from the University of Chicago (1988), and his PhD from Harvard University (1993). He is the author of *Obstinate Hebrews: Representations of Jews in France, 1715–1815* (Berkeley: University of California Press, 2003), for which he won awards from the Society for French Historical Studies and the American Historical Association. He is the editor of *The French Revolution: The Essential Readings* (Oxford: Blackwell, 2001), and the translator and editor of *Nathan the Wise by Gotthold Ephraim Lessing with Related Documents* (Boston and New York: St. Martin's Press, 2004). Since receiving his PhD he has received visiting fellowships from Ruprecht-Karls-Universität Heidelberg, the Shelby Cullom Davis Center for Historical Studies (Princeton University), and the Oxford Center for Hebrew and Jewish Studies (Oxford University).

ABOUT THE ILLUSTRATOR

Liz Clarke is an illustrator based in Cape Town, South Africa. Her artwork has appeared in magazines, games, and books, including *Abina and the Important Men* (OUP, 2011).

A NOTE ON HEBREW LETTERS...

Each of this book's five parts opens with a Hebrew letter. Together the letters spell the name "Daniel," which is pronounced DAHN-EE-*EL* in Hebrew. The first letter (ד) is called a "dalet" and has the sound of the "d" consonant. The second letter (נ) is called a "nun" and has the sound of the "n" consonant. The third letter (י) is called a "yud" and corresponds to the "y" in English but sounds like the vowel "ee" in DAHN-*EE*-EL. The fourth letter (א) is called an "aleph" and by itself is silent but carries the short "e" vowel in DAHN-EE-*EL*. The fifth letter (ל) is called a "lamed" and corresponds to the "l" consonant in English. (The "a" in Daniel is not indicated by a Hebrew letter.)

Hebrew is written from right to left, so the name "Daniel" looks like this:

דניאל

PART I
THE GRAPHIC HISTORY

ז

CHAPTER 1
THE MAKING OF A BOXER

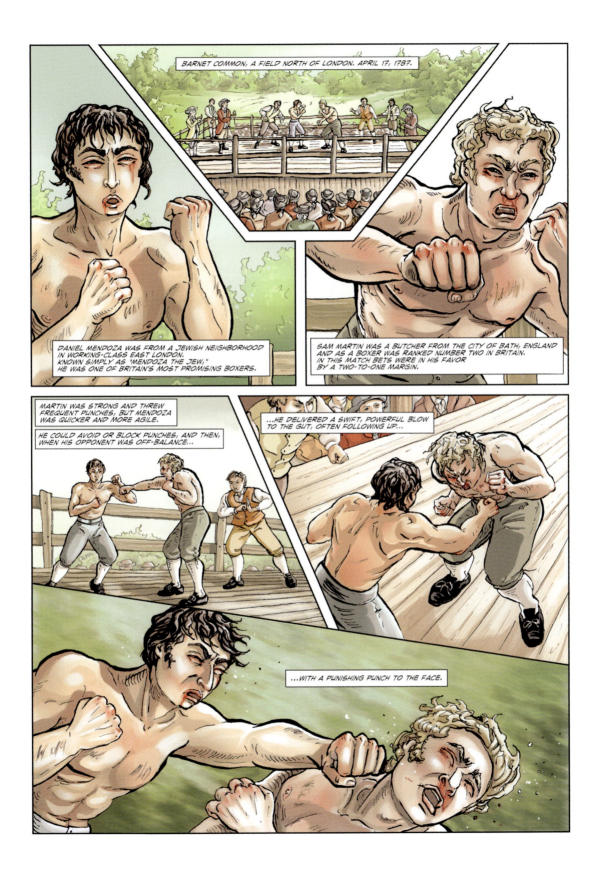

BARNET COMMON, A FIELD NORTH OF LONDON. APRIL 17, 1787.

DANIEL MENDOZA WAS FROM A JEWISH NEIGHBORHOOD IN WORKING-CLASS EAST LONDON.
KNOWN SIMPLY AS "MENDOZA THE JEW," HE WAS ONE OF BRITAIN'S MOST PROMISING BOXERS.

SAM MARTIN WAS A BUTCHER FROM THE CITY OF BATH, ENGLAND AND AS A BOXER WAS RANKED NUMBER TWO IN BRITAIN.
IN THIS MATCH BETS WERE IN HIS FAVOR BY A TWO-TO-ONE MARGIN.

MARTIN WAS STRONG AND THREW FREQUENT PUNCHES, BUT MENDOZA WAS QUICKER AND MORE AGILE.

HE COULD AVOID OR BLOCK PUNCHES, AND THEN, WHEN HIS OPPONENT WAS OFF-BALANCE...

...HE DELIVERED A SWIFT, POWERFUL BLOW TO THE GUT, OFTEN FOLLOWING UP...

...WITH A PUNISHING PUNCH TO THE FACE.

5

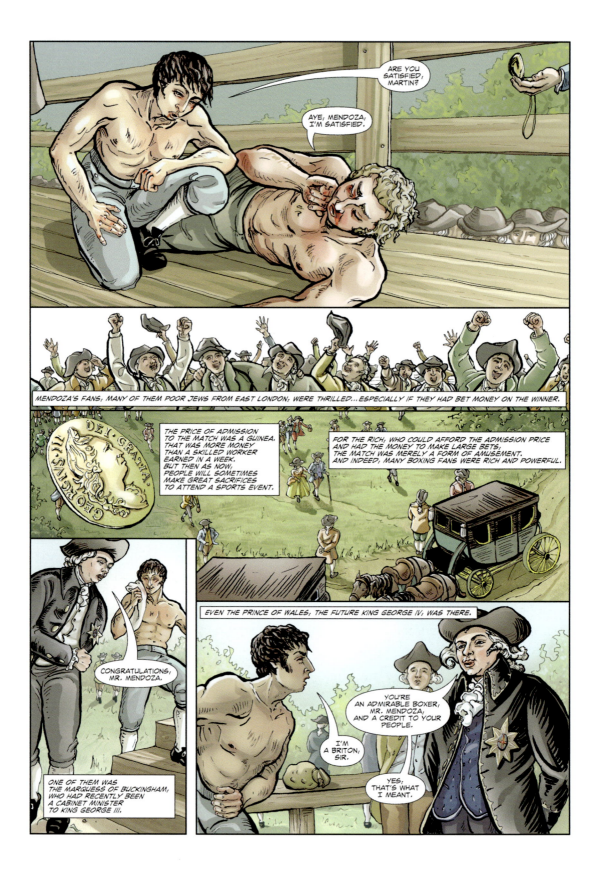

ARE YOU SATISFIED, MARTIN?

AYE, MENDOZA, I'M SATISFIED.

MENDOZA'S FANS, MANY OF THEM POOR JEWS FROM EAST LONDON, WERE THRILLED...ESPECIALLY IF THEY HAD BET MONEY ON THE WINNER.

THE PRICE OF ADMISSION TO THE MATCH WAS A GUINEA. THAT WAS MORE MONEY THAN A SKILLED WORKER EARNED IN A WEEK. BUT THEN AS NOW, PEOPLE WILL SOMETIMES MAKE GREAT SACRIFICES TO ATTEND A SPORTS EVENT.

FOR THE RICH, WHO COULD AFFORD THE ADMISSION PRICE AND HAD THE MONEY TO MAKE LARGE BETS, THE MATCH WAS MERELY A FORM OF AMUSEMENT. AND INDEED, MANY BOXING FANS WERE RICH AND POWERFUL.

EVEN THE PRINCE OF WALES, THE FUTURE KING GEORGE IV, WAS THERE.

CONGRATULATIONS, MR. MENDOZA.

ONE OF THEM WAS THE MARQUESS OF BUCKINGHAM, WHO HAD RECENTLY BEEN A CABINET MINISTER TO KING GEORGE III.

YOU'RE AN ADMIRABLE BOXER, MR. MENDOZA, AND A CREDIT TO YOUR PEOPLE.

I'M A BRITON, SIR.

YES, THAT'S WHAT I MEANT.

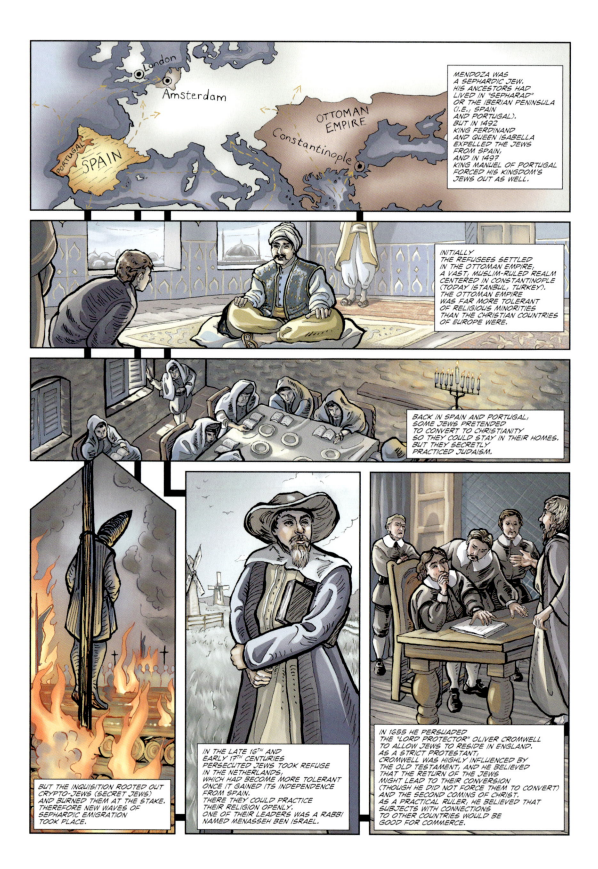

MENDOZA WAS A SEPHARDIC JEW. HIS ANCESTORS HAD LIVED IN "SEPHARAD" OR THE IBERIAN PENINSULA (I.E., SPAIN AND PORTUGAL). BUT IN 1492 KING FERDINAND AND QUEEN ISABELLA EXPELLED THE JEWS FROM SPAIN; AND IN 1497 KING MANUEL OF PORTUGAL FORCED HIS KINGDOM'S JEWS OUT AS WELL.

INITIALLY THE REFUGEES SETTLED IN THE OTTOMAN EMPIRE, A VAST, MUSLIM-RULED REALM CENTERED IN CONSTANTINOPLE (TODAY ISTANBUL, TURKEY). THE OTTOMAN EMPIRE WAS FAR MORE TOLERANT OF RELIGIOUS MINORITIES THAN THE CHRISTIAN COUNTRIES OF EUROPE WERE.

BACK IN SPAIN AND PORTUGAL, SOME JEWS PRETENDED TO CONVERT TO CHRISTIANITY SO THEY COULD STAY IN THEIR HOMES. BUT THEY SECRETLY PRACTICED JUDAISM.

BUT THE INQUISITION ROOTED OUT CRYPTO-JEWS (SECRET JEWS) AND BURNED THEM AT THE STAKE. THEREFORE NEW WAVES OF SEPHARDIC EMIGRATION TOOK PLACE.

IN THE LATE 16TH AND EARLY 17TH CENTURIES PERSECUTED JEWS TOOK REFUGE IN THE NETHERLANDS, WHICH HAD BECOME MORE TOLERANT ONCE IT GAINED ITS INDEPENDENCE FROM SPAIN. THERE THEY COULD PRACTICE THEIR RELIGION OPENLY. ONE OF THEIR LEADERS WAS A RABBI NAMED MENASSEH BEN ISRAEL.

IN 1655 HE PERSUADED THE "LORD PROTECTOR" OLIVER CROMWELL TO ALLOW JEWS TO RESIDE IN ENGLAND. AS A STRICT PROTESTANT, CROMWELL WAS HIGHLY INFLUENCED BY THE OLD TESTAMENT; AND HE BELIEVED THAT THE RETURN OF THE JEWS MIGHT LEAD TO THEIR CONVERSION (THOUGH HE DID NOT FORCE THEM TO CONVERT) AND THE SECOND COMING OF CHRIST. AS A PRACTICAL RULER, HE BELIEVED THAT SUBJECTS WITH CONNECTIONS TO OTHER COUNTRIES WOULD BE GOOD FOR COMMERCE.

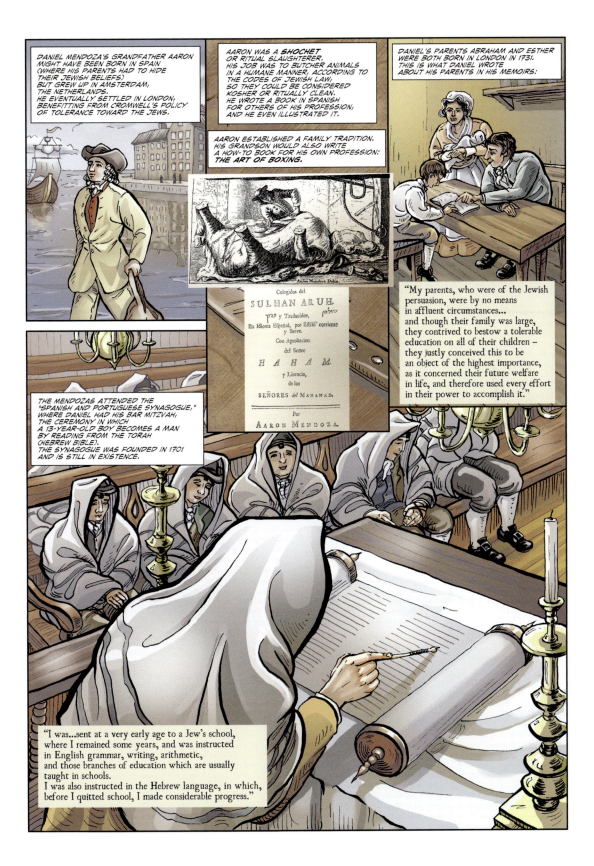

DANIEL MENDOZA'S GRANDFATHER AARON MIGHT HAVE BEEN BORN IN SPAIN (WHERE HIS PARENTS HAD TO HIDE THEIR JEWISH BELIEFS) BUT GREW UP IN AMSTERDAM, THE NETHERLANDS. HE EVENTUALLY SETTLED IN LONDON, BENEFITTING FROM CROMWELL'S POLICY OF TOLERANCE TOWARD THE JEWS.

AARON WAS A *SHOCHET* OR RITUAL SLAUGHTERER. HIS JOB WAS TO BUTCHER ANIMALS IN A HUMANE MANNER, ACCORDING TO THE CODES OF JEWISH LAW, SO THEY COULD BE CONSIDERED KOSHER OR RITUALLY CLEAN. HE WROTE A BOOK IN SPANISH FOR OTHERS OF HIS PROFESSION, AND HE EVEN ILLUSTRATED IT.

AARON ESTABLISHED A FAMILY TRADITION. HIS GRANDSON WOULD ALSO WRITE A HOW-TO BOOK FOR HIS OWN PROFESSION: *THE ART OF BOXING.*

DANIEL'S PARENTS ABRAHAM AND ESTHER WERE BOTH BORN IN LONDON IN 1731. THIS IS WHAT DANIEL WROTE ABOUT HIS PARENTS IN HIS MEMOIRS:

"My parents, who were of the Jewish persuasion, were by no means in affluent circumstances... and though their family was large, they contrived to bestow a tolerable education on all of their children – they justly conceived this to be an object of the highest importance, as it concerned their future welfare in life, and therefore used every effort in their power to accomplish it."

THE MENDOZAS ATTENDED THE "SPANISH AND PORTUGUESE SYNAGOGUE," WHERE DANIEL HAD HIS BAR MITZVAH, THE CEREMONY IN WHICH A 13-YEAR-OLD BOY BECOMES A MAN BY READING FROM THE TORAH (HEBREW BIBLE). THE SYNAGOGUE WAS FOUNDED IN 1701 AND IS STILL IN EXISTENCE.

"I was...sent at a very early age to a Jew's school, where I remained some years, and was instructed in English grammar, writing, arithmetic, and those branches of education which are usually taught in schools. I was also instructed in the Hebrew language, in which, before I quitted school, I made considerable progress."

9

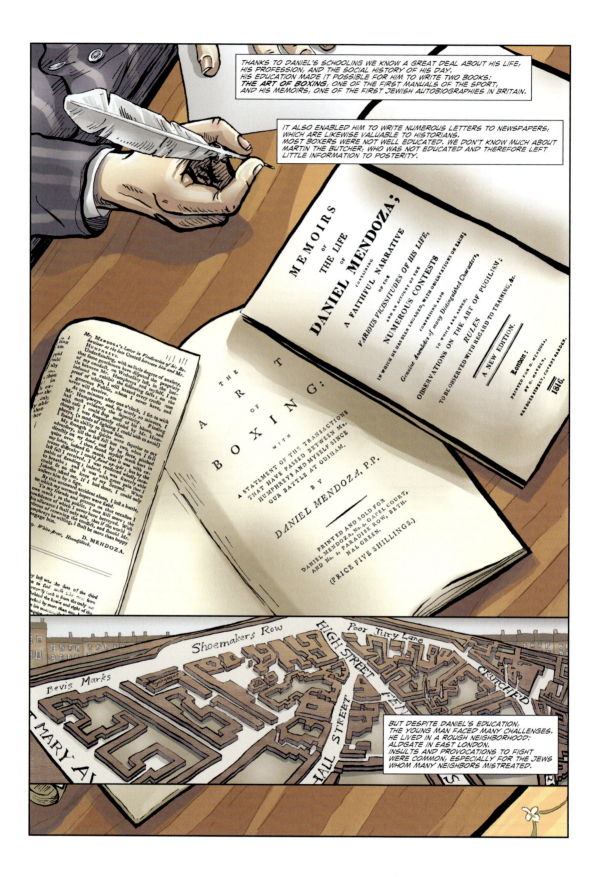

THANKS TO DANIEL'S SCHOOLING WE KNOW A GREAT DEAL ABOUT HIS LIFE, HIS PROFESSION, AND THE SOCIAL HISTORY OF HIS DAY.
HIS EDUCATION MADE IT POSSIBLE FOR HIM TO WRITE TWO BOOKS:
THE ART OF BOXING, ONE OF THE FIRST MANUALS OF THE SPORT,
AND HIS MEMOIRS, ONE OF THE FIRST JEWISH AUTOBIOGRAPHIES IN BRITAIN.

IT ALSO ENABLED HIM TO WRITE NUMEROUS LETTERS TO NEWSPAPERS, WHICH ARE LIKEWISE VALUABLE TO HISTORIANS.
MOST BOXERS WERE NOT WELL EDUCATED AND THEREFORE LEFT LITTLE INFORMATION TO POSTERITY. WE DON'T KNOW MUCH ABOUT MARTIN THE BUTCHER, WHO WAS NOT EDUCATED AND THEREFORE LEFT LITTLE INFORMATION TO POSTERITY.

MEMOIRS
OF
THE LIFE
OF
DANIEL MENDOZA;
CONTAINING
A FAITHFUL NARRATIVE
OF THE
VARIOUS VICISSITUDES OF HIS LIFE,
AND AN ACCOUNT OF THE
NUMEROUS CONTESTS
IN WHICH HE HAS BEEN ENGAGED, WITH OBSERVATIONS ON EACH;
COMPRISING ALSO
Genuine Anecdotes of many Distinguished Characters,
TO WHICH ARE ADDED,
OBSERVATIONS ON THE ART OF PUGILISM;
RULES
TO BE OBSERVED WITH REGARD TO TRAINING, &c.

A NEW EDITION.

London:
PRINTED FOR D. MENDOZA,
BY G. HAYDEN,
BRYDGES STREET, COVENT GARDEN.
1816.

THE
ART
OF
BOXING:
WITH
A STATEMENT OF THE TRANSACTIONS
THAT HAVE PASSED BETWEEN Mr.
HUMPHREYS AND MYSELF SINCE
OUR BATTLE AT ODIHAM.
BY
DANIEL MENDOZA, P.P.

PRINTED AND SOLD FOR
DANIEL MENDOZA, No. 2, GAPEL COURT,
AND No. 2, PARADISE ROW, BETH-
NAL GREEN.
(PRICE FIVE SHILLINGS.)

BUT DESPITE DANIEL'S EDUCATION, THE YOUNG MAN FACED MANY CHALLENGES. HE LIVED IN A ROUGH NEIGHBORHOOD: ALDGATE IN EAST LONDON.
INSULTS AND PROVOCATIONS TO FIGHT WERE COMMON, ESPECIALLY FOR THE JEWS WHOM MANY NEIGHBORS MISTREATED.

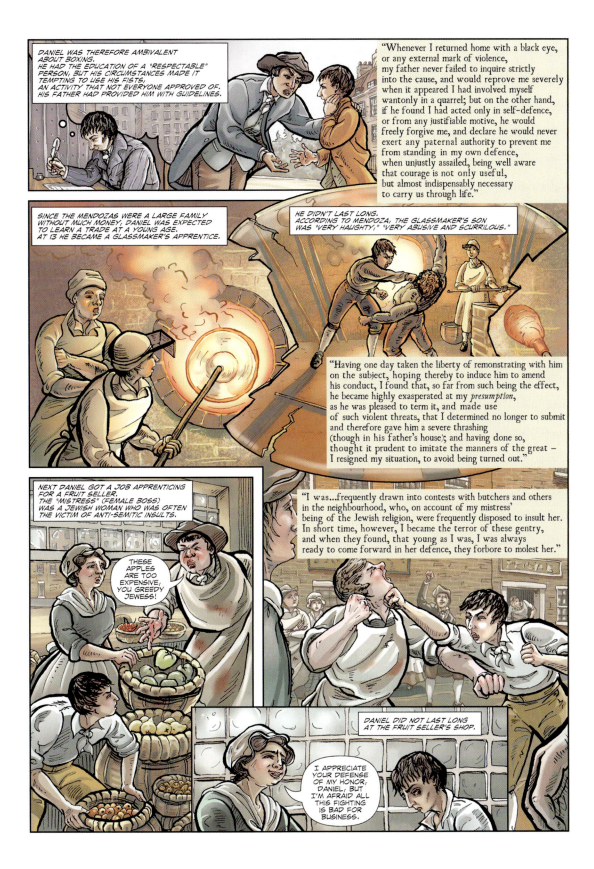

DANIEL WAS THEREFORE AMBIVALENT ABOUT BOXING.
HE HAD THE EDUCATION OF A "RESPECTABLE" PERSON, BUT HIS CIRCUMSTANCES MADE IT TEMPTING TO USE HIS FISTS, AN ACTIVITY THAT NOT EVERYONE APPROVED OF.
HIS FATHER HAD PROVIDED HIM WITH GUIDELINES.

"Whenever I returned home with a black eye, or any external mark of violence, my father never failed to inquire strictly into the cause, and would reprove me severely when it appeared I had involved myself wantonly in a quarrel; but on the other hand, if he found I had acted only in self-defence, or from any justifiable motive, he would freely forgive me, and declare he would never exert any paternal authority to prevent me from standing in my own defence, when unjustly assailed, being well aware that courage is not only useful, but almost indispensably necessary to carry us through life."

SINCE THE MENDOZAS WERE A LARGE FAMILY WITHOUT MUCH MONEY, DANIEL WAS EXPECTED TO LEARN A TRADE AT A YOUNG AGE.
AT 13 HE BECAME A GLASSMAKER'S APPRENTICE.

HE DIDN'T LAST LONG.
ACCORDING TO MENDOZA, THE GLASSMAKER'S SON WAS "VERY HAUGHTY," "VERY ABUSIVE AND SCURRILOUS."

"Having one day taken the liberty of remonstrating with him on the subject, hoping thereby to induce him to amend his conduct, I found that, so far from such being the effect, he became highly exasperated at my *presumption*, as he was pleased to term it, and made use of such violent threats, that I determined no longer to submit and therefore gave him a severe thrashing (though in his father's house); and having done so, thought it prudent to imitate the manners of the great – I resigned my situation, to avoid being turned out."

NEXT DANIEL GOT A JOB APPRENTICING FOR A FRUIT SELLER.
THE "MISTRESS" (FEMALE BOSS) WAS A JEWISH WOMAN WHO WAS OFTEN THE VICTIM OF ANTI-SEMITIC INSULTS.

THESE APPLES ARE TOO EXPENSIVE, YOU GREEDY JEWESS!

"I was...frequently drawn into contests with butchers and others in the neighbourhood, who, on account of my mistress' being of the Jewish religion, were frequently disposed to insult her. In short time, however, I became the terror of these gentry, and when they found, that young as I was, I was always ready to come forward in her defence, they forbore to molest her."

DANIEL DID NOT LAST LONG AT THE FRUIT SELLER'S SHOP.

I APPRECIATE YOUR DEFENSE OF MY HONOR, DANIEL, BUT I'M AFRAID ALL THIS FIGHTING IS BAD FOR BUSINESS.

DANIEL WENT FROM JOB TO JOB. HE WORKED FOR A TEA DEALER...

...AT A TOBACCONIST'S SHOP...

...IN A CANDY FACTORY...

...AS A COOKIE BAKER...

HE WAS EVEN A SMUGGLER FOR A FEW DAYS.

"...having learnt that one of our party had, but a few weeks previous to this, lost his life in an affray with some revenue officers, I quitted my employment in disgust, having remained therein only four or five days."

THE ONLY THING YOUNG DANIEL COULD DO CONSISTENTLY WAS FIGHT.

DANIEL FIRST RECEIVED MONEY FOR FIGHTING
IN THE SUMMER OF 1780, WHEN HE WAS ONLY 15 YEARS OLD.
AN UNNAMED "FRIEND" HAD ARRANGED
A BOXING MATCH FOR AN UNSPECIFIED SUM
IN MILE END ROAD.
IT TOOK PLACE ON A SATURDAY; "A DAY OF LEISURE FOR US,"
IN OTHER WORDS, THE JEWISH SABBATH.
DANIEL DID NOT WORK ON THAT DAY – HE WAS STILL
AN EMPLOYEE OF THE TEA DEALER THEN – BUT HE DID NOT
SEE BOXING AS A VIOLATION OF THE SABBATH.

DANIEL WAS NOW
A PROFESSIONAL
BOXER.
HE WAS EARNING
MONEY FOR PUNCHING
ANOTHER MAN INTO
SUBMISSION.
HE WAS NOT AVENGING
AN INSULT OR FIGHTING
IN SELF-DEFENSE.
THERE ARE NO
RECORDS OF WHAT
HIS FATHER THOUGHT,
BUT IN HIS MEMOIRS
DANIEL IS SOMEWHAT
DEFENSIVE.

"I had never before
fought for money,
and felt some reluctance
to a battle of that sort
on the present occasion;
however, as my friend
had made the match,
I was unwilling
to disappoint him,
and therefore resolved
to use my utmost
exertions in his favour."

"Accordingly,
at the time appointed,
I met my opponent,
and...had to contend
against superior strength;
but, after a contest
which lasted near an hour,
had the satisfaction
to...come off victorious."

IN THE EIGHTEENTH CENTURY BOXERS
DID NOT ENTER THE RING ALONE.
EACH HAD A "SECOND" AND A
"BOTTLE-HOLDER."
THE SECOND WAS OFTEN A MORE
EXPERIENCED BOXER WHO FUNCTIONED
AS A KIND OF COACH.
IN 1780 DANIEL'S SECOND WAS
AN UP-AND-COMING BOXER NAMED
RICHARD HUMPHRIES (SOMETIMES
SPELLED HUMPHREYS).

"Mr. Humphreys was...my second on this occasion;
and when some of the spectators called out to him
to direct me where to strike, I well recollect
hearing him reply, 'there is no need of it, the lad
knows more than us all.'"

DID MENDOZA IMAGINE THIS EXCHANGE?
WE CAN'T KNOW FOR CERTAIN.
BUT WHATEVER RICHARD HUMPHRIES SAID ON THAT OCCASION,
THE HARMONY BETWEEN THE TWO MEN
WAS NOT DESTINED TO LAST.

CHAPTER 2

BOXING LESSONS

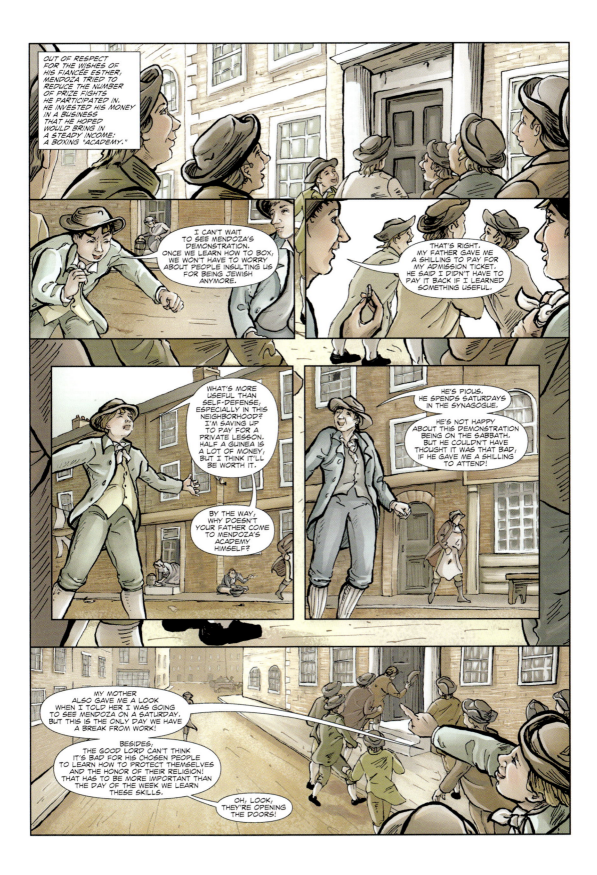

OUT OF RESPECT FOR THE WISHES OF HIS FIANCÉE ESTHER, MENDOZA TRIED TO REDUCE THE NUMBER OF PRIZE FIGHTS HE PARTICIPATED IN. HE INVESTED HIS MONEY IN A BUSINESS THAT HE HOPED WOULD BRING IN A STEADY INCOME: A BOXING "ACADEMY."

I CAN'T WAIT TO SEE MENDOZA'S DEMONSTRATION. ONCE WE LEARN HOW TO BOX, WE WON'T HAVE TO WORRY ABOUT PEOPLE INSULTING US FOR BEING JEWISH ANYMORE.

THAT'S RIGHT. MY FATHER GAVE ME A SHILLING TO PAY FOR MY ADMISSION TICKET. HE SAID I DIDN'T HAVE TO PAY IT BACK IF I LEARNED SOMETHING USEFUL.

WHAT'S MORE USEFUL THAN SELF-DEFENSE, ESPECIALLY IN THIS NEIGHBORHOOD? I'M SAVING UP TO PAY FOR A PRIVATE LESSON. HALF A GUINEA IS A LOT OF MONEY, BUT I THINK IT'LL BE WORTH IT.

BY THE WAY, WHY DOESN'T YOUR FATHER COME TO MENDOZA'S ACADEMY HIMSELF?

HE'S PIOUS. HE SPENDS SATURDAYS IN THE SYNAGOGUE.

HE'S NOT HAPPY ABOUT THIS DEMONSTRATION BEING ON THE SABBATH, BUT HE COULDN'T HAVE THOUGHT IT WAS THAT BAD, IF HE GAVE ME A SHILLING TO ATTEND!

MY MOTHER ALSO GAVE ME A LOOK WHEN I TOLD HER I WAS GOING TO SEE MENDOZA ON A SATURDAY. BUT THIS IS THE ONLY DAY WE HAVE A BREAK FROM WORK!

BESIDES, THE GOOD LORD CAN'T THINK IT'S BAD FOR HIS CHOSEN PEOPLE TO LEARN HOW TO PROTECT THEMSELVES AND THE HONOR OF THEIR RELIGION! THAT HAS TO BE MORE IMPORTANT THAN THE DAY OF THE WEEK WE LEARN THESE SKILLS.

OH, LOOK, THEY'RE OPENING THE DOORS!

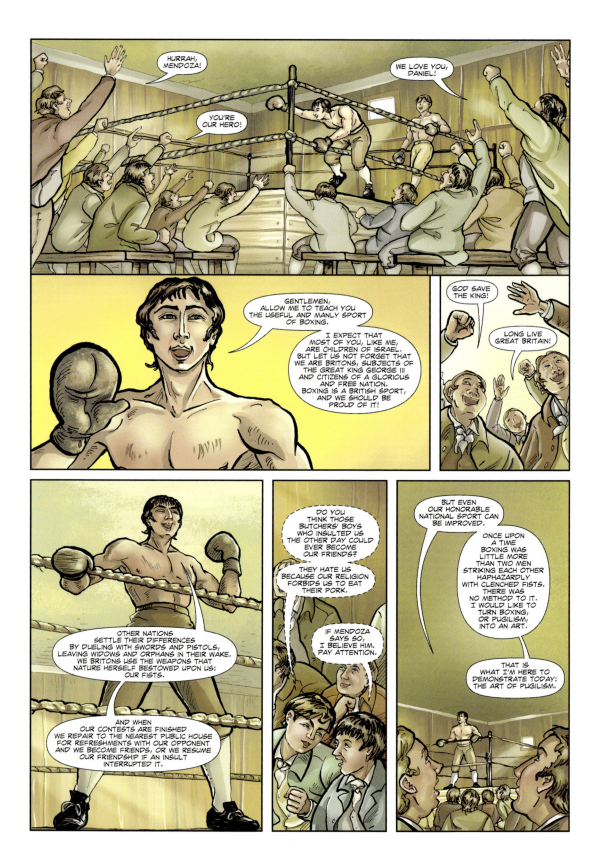

18

THE PRINCIPLES OF BOXING ARE SIMPLE.

THE FIRST IS BALANCE. YOU SHOULD BE ABLE TO CHANGE FROM A RIGHT-HAND TO A LEFT-HAND POSITION; YOU SHOULD BE ABLE TO ADVANCE OR RETREAT WHILE STRIKING YOUR OPPONENT OR PARRYING HIS BLOW; AND YOU SHOULD BE ABLE TO MOVE YOUR BODY FORWARD OR BACKWARD WITH SPEED AND EASE.

WITH PRACTICE YOU CAN DO ALL THESE THINGS WITHOUT LOSING YOUR BALANCE.

THE SECOND PRINCIPLE IS THAT OF KEEPING YOUR BODY IN A DIAGONAL POSITION.

THE MAIN THING HERE IS TO KEEP THE PIT OF YOUR STOMACH OUT OF YOUR ADVERSARY'S REACH. OF COURSE, THIS POSITION WILL LEAVE YOUR HEAD VULNERABLE, SO YOU HAVE TO LEARN TO PARRY; IN OTHER WORDS STOP, WITH THE UPPER PART OF YOUR ARM ANY ROUND BLOWS AIMED AT YOUR HEAD.

YOU WILL USE YOUR FOREARM TO PARRY YOUR OPPONENT'S BLOWS TO THE FACE OR STOMACH; AND YOU WILL USE YOUR ELBOWS TO STOP YOUR ADVERSARY FROM HITTING YOU IN THE RIBS.

ALSO, KEEP YOUR KNEES BENT, PLACE YOUR LEFT LEG FORWARD, AND KEEP YOUR ARMS DIRECTLY IN FRONT OF YOUR THROAT OR CHIN.

I THOUGHT HE SAID IT WOULD BE SIMPLE. I'M HAVING TROUBLE FOLLOWING.

BUT IT'S AN ART. I THINK I UNDERSTAND. TRY TO PAY CLOSER ATTENTION.

I HEAR A BIT OF MURMURING. PERHAPS SOME OF YOU ARE CONFUSED.

LET ME TEACH YOU ANOTHER PRINCIPLE. AND THEN I'LL DEMONSTRATE WITH MY BROTHER. WHEN YOU SEE THESE PRINCIPLES IN ACTION, THEY WILL BE EASIER TO UNDERSTAND.

HERE'S SOMETHING YOU MUST ALWAYS KEEP IN MIND. WHENEVER YOUR OPPONENT TRIES TO STRIKE YOU WITH HIS RIGHT HAND, YOU MUST PARRY THE BLOW WITH YOUR LEFT ARM. AND WHENEVER HE TRIES TO STRIKE YOU WITH HIS LEFT HAND, YOU MUST PARRY THE BLOW WITH YOUR RIGHT ARM.

PARRY RIGHT WITH LEFT; PARRY LEFT WITH RIGHT. DO YOU FOLLOW? BUT DON'T FORGET TO GUARD YOUR STOMACH WITH THE ARM YOU'RE NOT USING TO STRIKE OR PARRY.

BUT LET'S SWITCH FROM THEORY TO PRACTICE.

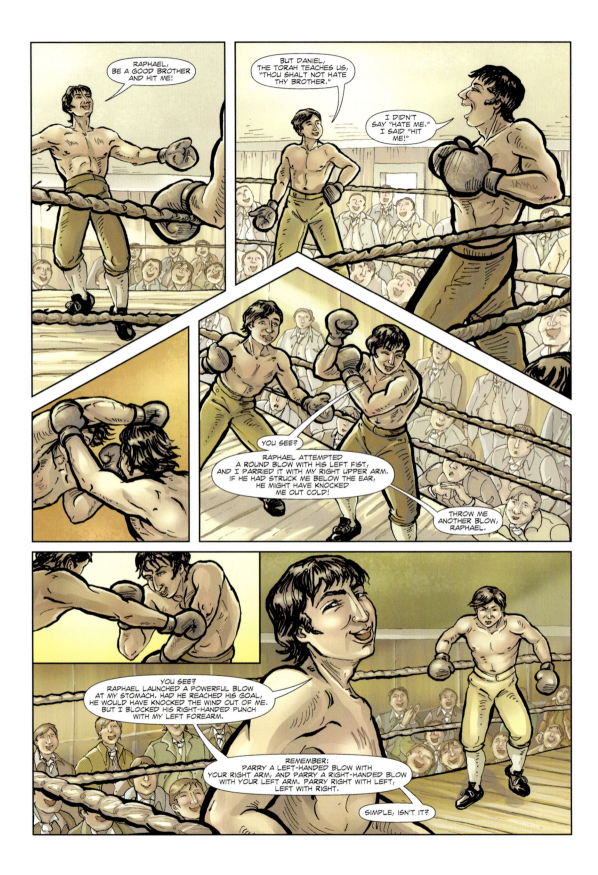

OTHER NATIONS SETTLE THEIR DIFFERENCES BY DUELING WITH SWORDS AND PISTOLS, LEAVING WIDOWS AND ORPHANS IN THEIR WAKE.

WE BRITONS USE THE WEAPONS THAT NATURE HERSELF BESTOWED UPON US: OUR FISTS.

THINGS WERE LOOKING UP FOR DANIEL AND ESTHER, WHO WERE MARRIED ON MAY 22, 1787. THEN, ONE DAY...

MR. MENDOZA? I'M AFRAID I HAVE A WARRANT FOR YOUR ARREST.

I DON'T UNDERSTAND. I HAVEN'T DONE ANYTHING UNLAWFUL.

A CERTAIN MR. REYNOLDS HAS ACCUSED YOU OF TAKING TWENTY GUINEAS FROM HIM AND FAILING TO REPAY HIM.

MR. REYNOLDS GAVE ME A *GIFT* OF TWENTY GUINEAS.

HE WON THE MONEY BETTING ON ME IN MY CONTEST WITH MARTIN THE BUTCHER, AND AFTERWARDS HE GAVE IT TO ME AS A *PRESENT*.

SAVE YOUR DEFENSE FOR THE MAGISTRATE, MR. MENDOZA. YOU WILL HAVE YOUR CHANCE TO TELL YOUR SIDE OF THE STORY.

23

AND IF HE'S NOT,
ARE YOU GOING TO LET
YOURSELF BE TRICKED
INTO FIGHTING A MATCH
THAT YOU KNOW
I DON'T WANT?

CHAPTER 3

ODIHAM

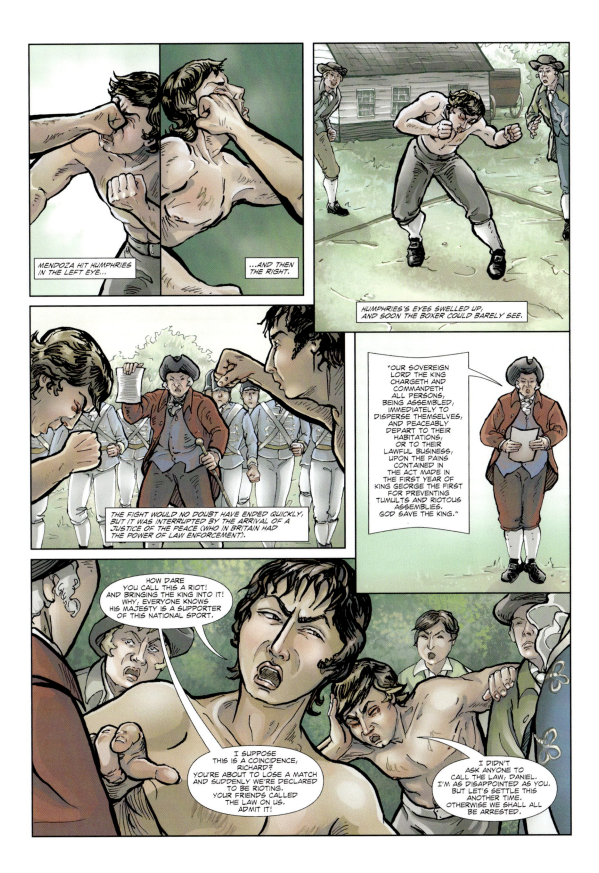

MENDOZA HIT HUMPHRIES IN THE LEFT EYE...

...AND THEN THE RIGHT.

HUMPHRIES'S EYES SWELLED UP, AND SOON THE BOXER COULD BARELY SEE.

THE FIGHT WOULD NO DOUBT HAVE ENDED QUICKLY, BUT IT WAS INTERRUPTED BY THE ARRIVAL OF A JUSTICE OF THE PEACE (WHO IN BRITAIN HAD THE POWER OF LAW ENFORCEMENT).

"OUR SOVEREIGN LORD THE KING CHARGETH AND COMMANDETH ALL PERSONS, BEING ASSEMBLED, IMMEDIATELY TO DISPERSE THEMSELVES, AND PEACEABLY DEPART TO THEIR HABITATIONS, OR TO THEIR LAWFUL BUSINESS, UPON THE PAINS CONTAINED IN THE ACT MADE IN THE FIRST YEAR OF KING GEORGE THE FIRST FOR PREVENTING TUMULTS AND RIOTOUS ASSEMBLIES. GOD SAVE THE KING."

HOW DARE YOU CALL THIS A RIOT! AND BRINGING THE KING INTO IT! WHY, EVERYONE KNOWS HIS MAJESTY IS A SUPPORTER OF THIS NATIONAL SPORT.

I SUPPOSE THIS IS A COINCIDENCE, RICHARD? YOU'RE ABOUT TO LOSE A MATCH AND SUDDENLY WE'RE DECLARED TO BE RIOTING. YOUR FRIENDS CALLED THE LAW ON US. ADMIT IT!

I DIDN'T ASK ANYONE TO CALL THE LAW, DANIEL. I'M AS DISAPPOINTED AS YOU. BUT LET'S SETTLE THIS ANOTHER TIME. OTHERWISE WE SHALL ALL BE ARRESTED.

MENDOZA AND HUMPHRIES MET AT THE SPREAD EAGLE PUB ON GRACECHURCH STREET, IN EAST LONDON, TO NEGOTIATE THE CONDITIONS OF THEIR IMPENDING MATCH. IN HIS MEMOIRS MENDOZA WROTE:

"It was settled...at this meeting that Mr. HUMPHREYS and myself should decide our contest on the 9th of January following, at Odiham in Hampshire; and it being probable that this battle would excite considerable interest among the amateurs and patrons of the pugilistic art, it was agreed that we should fight in an inclosed space in an inn yard, that half a guinea should be the price of admission for spectators, and that the money should be divided between us."

THE "STAKES," LITERALLY A BAG OF COINS HANGING FROM A STAKE AT THE EDGE OF THE RING, WOULD AMOUNT TO 50 GUINEAS, 25 OF WHICH WOULD BE PROVIDED BY EACH OF THE BOXERS (OR THEIR "BACKERS").

BUT THIS WAS ONLY A FRACTION OF THE EXPECTED "GATE MONEY" TO BE DIVIDED BETWEEN THE CONTESTANTS REGARDLESS OF THE VICTOR. AND AS ALWAYS THE WINNER COULD EXPECT LARGE GIFTS FROM HIS WEALTHY FANS.

THE BOXERS KEPT THE LOCATION OF THE FIGHT A WELL-GUARDED SECRET UNTIL SHORTLY BEFORE THE MATCH, SO LOCAL LAW ENFORCEMENT OFFICIALS WOULD HAVE LESS TIME TO PREPARE TO STOP THE CONTEST IN CASE THEY DEEMED IT A "RIOT."

NEWSPAPERS SPECULATED ON THE LOCATION, BUT MOST WERE INCORRECT. ONE PAPER NARROWED IT DOWN TO BRIGHTHELMSTONE IN SUSSEX OR MARGATE IN KENT. ANOTHER CLAIMED COLCHESTER IN ESSEX AS THE SITE OF THE PROPOSED MATCH. YET ANOTHER WAS CERTAIN THE FIGHT WOULD BE "AT OR NEAR NEWBURY, IN BERKSHIRE."

HUMPHRIES TRAINED HARD WITH HIS FRIEND LOCKIT, THE APTLY NAMED JAILOR (GAOLER) OF THE TOWN OF IPSWICH.

MENDOZA DIDN'T FEEL HE NEEDED TO TRAIN:

"Notwithstanding my most ardent expectations were fixed on the event of this battle, I paid no more regard to training on this than on any former occasion, having sufficient confidence in my natural activity and the excellence of my constitution, and therefore passed the interval without varying in any way my usual mode of living."

MENDOZA'S MAIN PHYSICAL ACTIVITY WAS FOX HUNTING, BUT THIS WAS MORE FOR SOCIALIZING WITH RICH MEN THAN FOR EXERCISE. YET HE DIDN'T FIT IN WITH THE ARISTOCRATS, AND HE MADE ERRORS SUCH AS "RIDING AMONG THE HOUNDS."

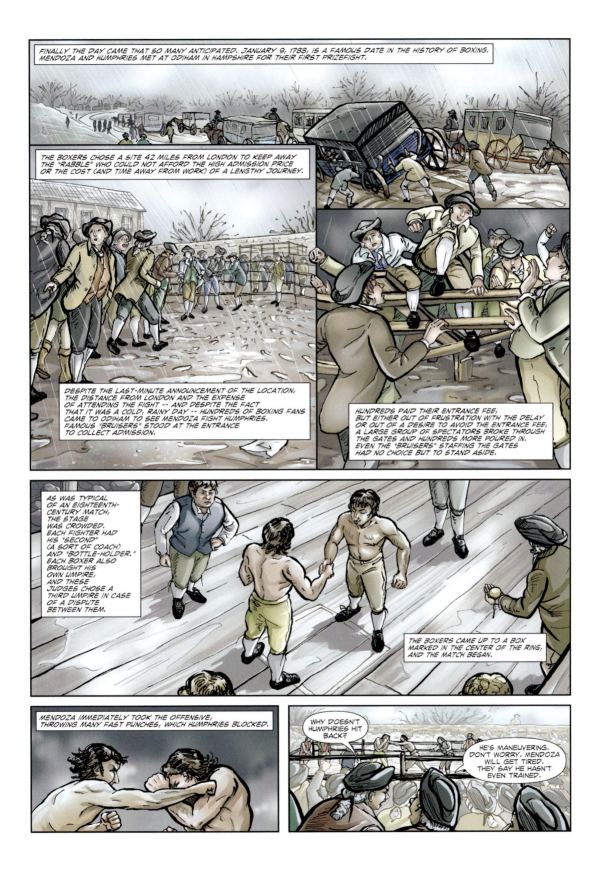

FINALLY THE DAY CAME THAT SO MANY ANTICIPATED. JANUARY 9, 1788, IS A FAMOUS DATE IN THE HISTORY OF BOXING. MENDOZA AND HUMPHRIES MET AT ODIHAM IN HAMPSHIRE FOR THEIR FIRST PRIZEFIGHT.

THE BOXERS CHOSE A SITE 42 MILES FROM LONDON TO KEEP AWAY THE "RABBLE" WHO COULD NOT AFFORD THE HIGH ADMISSION PRICE OR THE COST (AND TIME AWAY FROM WORK) OF A LENGTHY JOURNEY.

DESPITE THE LAST-MINUTE ANNOUNCEMENT OF THE LOCATION, THE DISTANCE FROM LONDON AND THE EXPENSE OF ATTENDING THE FIGHT -- AND DESPITE THE FACT THAT IT WAS A COLD, RAINY DAY -- HUNDREDS OF BOXING FANS CAME TO ODIHAM TO SEE MENDOZA FIGHT HUMPHRIES. FAMOUS "BRUISERS" STOOD AT THE ENTRANCE TO COLLECT ADMISSION.

HUNDREDS PAID THEIR ENTRANCE FEE, BUT EITHER OUT OF FRUSTRATION WITH THE DELAY OR OUT OF A DESIRE TO AVOID THE ENTRANCE FEE, A LARGE GROUP OF SPECTATORS BROKE THROUGH THE GATES AND HUNDREDS MORE POURED IN. EVEN THE "BRUISERS" STAFFING THE GATES HAD NO CHOICE BUT TO STAND ASIDE.

AS WAS TYPICAL OF AN EIGHTEENTH-CENTURY MATCH, THE STAGE WAS CROWDED. EACH FIGHTER HAD HIS "SECOND" (A SORT OF COACH) AND "BOTTLE-HOLDER." EACH BOXER ALSO BROUGHT HIS OWN UMPIRE, AND THESE JUDGES CHOSE A THIRD UMPIRE IN CASE OF A DISPUTE BETWEEN THEM.

THE BOXERS CAME UP TO A BOX MARKED IN THE CENTER OF THE RING, AND THE MATCH BEGAN.

MENDOZA IMMEDIATELY TOOK THE OFFENSIVE, THROWING MANY FAST PUNCHES, WHICH HUMPHRIES BLOCKED.

WHY DOESN'T HUMPHRIES HIT BACK?

HE'S MANEUVERING. DON'T WORRY. MENDOZA WILL GET TIRED. THEY SAY HE HASN'T EVEN TRAINED.

FOR FIFTEEN MINUTES MENDOZA REMAINED ON THE ATTACK.

AFTER ONE OF MENDOZA'S PUNCHES HUMPHRIES FELL BACK AGAINST THE RAILS.

MENDOZA WAS ABOUT TO FINISH HIS OPPONENT OFF WHEN...

...HUMPHRIES'S SECOND, JOHNSON, STEPPED IN AND BLOCKED THE PUNCH.

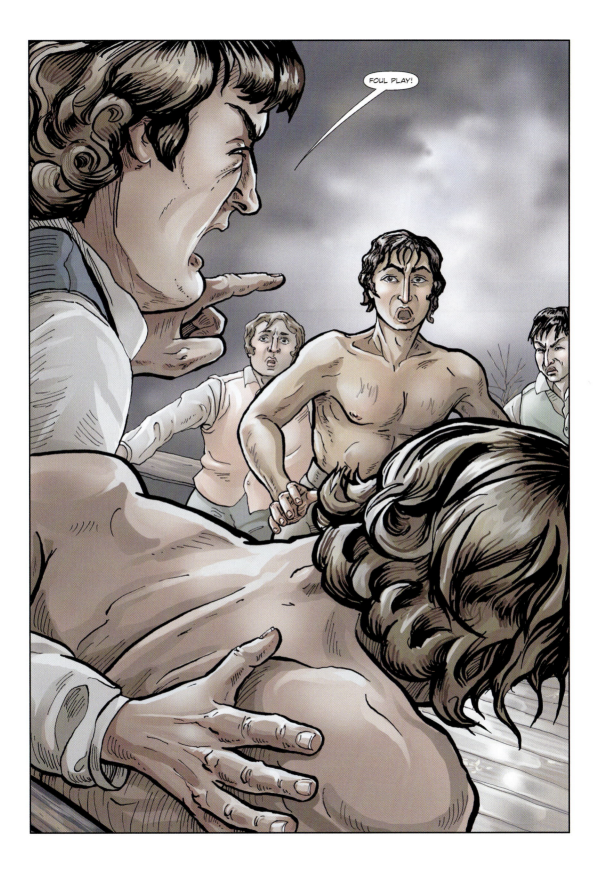

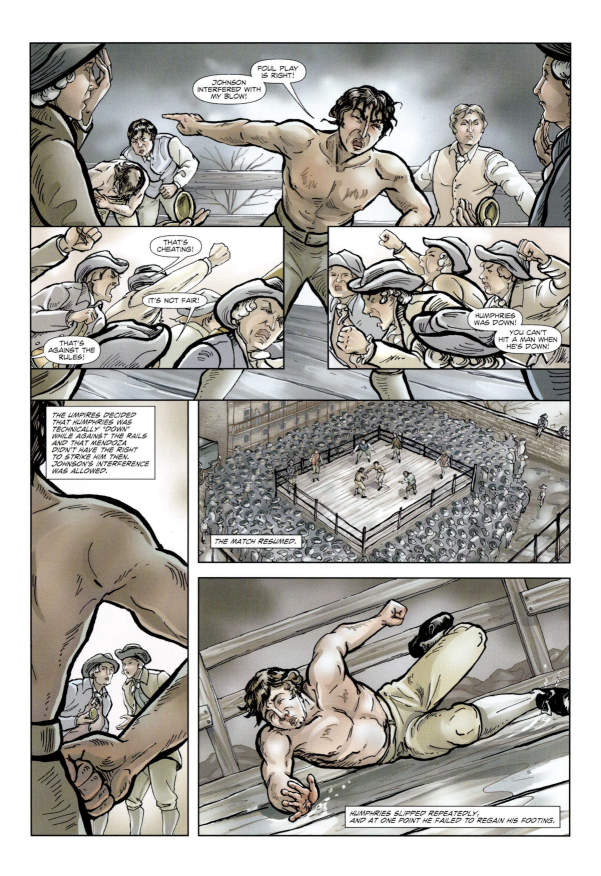

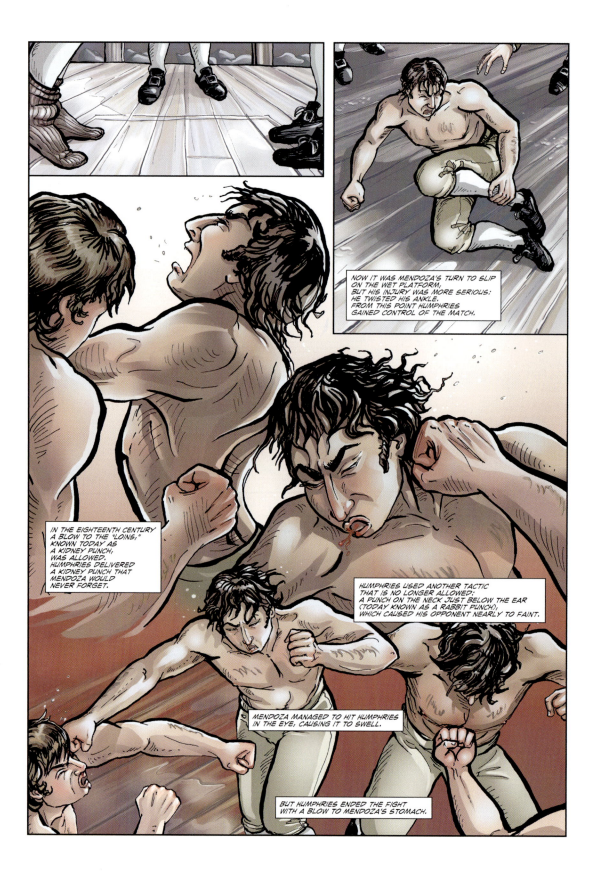

NOW IT WAS MENDOZA'S TURN TO SLIP
ON THE WET PLATFORM,
BUT HIS INJURY WAS MORE SERIOUS:
HE TWISTED HIS ANKLE.
FROM THIS POINT HUMPHRIES
GAINED CONTROL OF THE MATCH.

IN THE EIGHTEENTH CENTURY
A BLOW TO THE "LOINS,"
KNOWN TODAY AS
A KIDNEY PUNCH,
WAS ALLOWED.
HUMPHRIES DELIVERED
A KIDNEY PUNCH THAT
MENDOZA WOULD
NEVER FORGET.

HUMPHRIES USED ANOTHER TACTIC
THAT IS NO LONGER ALLOWED:
A PUNCH ON THE NECK JUST BELOW THE EAR
(TODAY KNOWN AS A RABBIT PUNCH),
WHICH CAUSED HIS OPPONENT NEARLY TO FAINT.

MENDOZA MANAGED TO HIT HUMPHRIES
IN THE EYE, CAUSING IT TO SWELL.

BUT HUMPHRIES ENDED THE FIGHT
WITH A BLOW TO MENDOZA'S STOMACH.

CHAPTER 4
STILTON

FOR THOSE WHO COULD NOT MAKE THE TRIP TO ODIHAM, IMAGES AND OBJECTS GAVE THEM SOME SENSE OF THE EXPERIENCE. ARTISTS SUCH AS JOHN HOPPNER, WHO HAD BEEN PRESENT AT THE ODIHAM FIGHT, PAINTED OR DREW THE ANTAGONISTS.

PAINTINGS SUCH AS HOPPNER'S WERE WIDELY SOLD IN PRINT FORM.

THE PRINTMAKER JAMES GILLRAY, BEST KNOWN TO HISTORY FOR HIS CARICATURES OF NAPOLEON, MADE A PRINT OF THE ODIHAM MATCH. IT CAPTURES THE MOMENT AT WHICH JOHNSON STOPPED MENDOZA'S PUNCH AND CLAIMS THAT MENDOZA WAS GUILTY OF "FOUL PLAY."

AND I HAVE THIS AMUSING LITTLE REPRESENTATION BY MR. GILLRAY.

A CERAMICS FACTORY IN STAFFORDSHIRE MADE COMMEMORATIVE MUGS.

ACTORS REPLACED THEIR SCRIPTED LINES WITH REFERENCES TO THE RECENT MATCH. AND SOME OF THEM ACTED OUT THE FIGHT IN PANTOMIME.

BUT THE MOST EFFICIENT MEANS OF CONVEYING INFORMATION AND OPINIONS ABOUT THE MATCH WAS THROUGH THE PRESS. MILLIONS OF BRITONS OBTAINED THEIR NEWS THROUGH HUNDREDS OF NEWSPAPERS AND MAGAZINES.

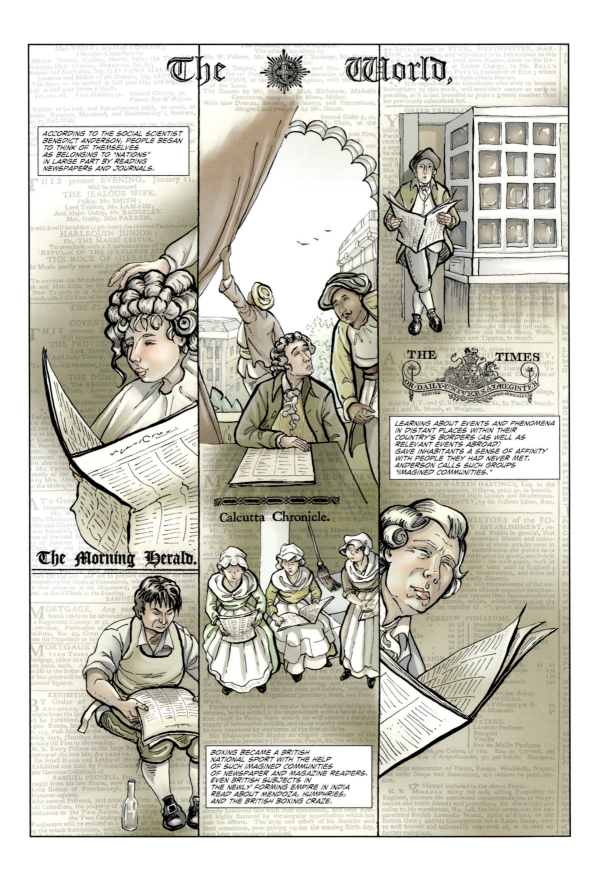

The World,

ACCORDING TO THE SOCIAL SCIENTIST BENEDICT ANDERSON, PEOPLE BEGAN TO THINK OF THEMSELVES AS BELONGING TO "NATIONS" IN LARGE PART BY READING NEWSPAPERS AND JOURNALS.

LEARNING ABOUT EVENTS AND PHENOMENA IN DISTANT PLACES WITHIN THEIR COUNTRY'S BORDERS (AS WELL AS RELEVANT EVENTS ABROAD) GAVE INHABITANTS A SENSE OF AFFINITY WITH PEOPLE THEY HAD NEVER MET. ANDERSON CALLS SUCH GROUPS "IMAGINED COMMUNITIES."

Calcutta Chronicle.

The Morning Herald.

BOXING BECAME A BRITISH NATIONAL SPORT WITH THE HELP OF SUCH IMAGINED COMMUNITIES OF NEWSPAPER AND MAGAZINE READERS. EVEN BRITISH SUBJECTS IN THE NEWLY FORMING EMPIRE IN INDIA READ ABOUT MENDOZA, HUMPHRIES, AND THE BRITISH BOXING CRAZE.

THE NEWSPAPERS PRINTED EVERYTHING THEY COULD FIND ABOUT THE MENDOZA-HUMPHRIES RIVALRY. MENDOZA KNEW THIS, AND HE USED THE PRESS TO VINDICATE HIS REPUTATION. TWO DAYS AFTER THE MATCH, HE WROTE A LETTER TO SEVERAL LONDON PAPERS CLAIMING THAT ONLY THE "ACCIDENT" OF A SPRAINED ANKLE HAD PREVENTED HIM FROM WINNING THE ODIHAM MATCH.

BY THIS UNTOWARD ACCIDENT ALONE, I LOST A BATTLE, ON WHICH MY WARMEST HOPES WERE FIXED.

REALLY! AN "ACCIDENT"!

LIKE MENDOZA, HUMPHRIES WAS UNUSUAL AMONG BOXERS IN HIS ABILITY TO READ AND WRITE WELL. HE WASN'T GOING TO LET MENDOZA GET AWAY WITH EXCUSES. HE WROTE TO THE SAME PAPERS AS MENDOZA AND OFFERED HIS OPPONENT A REMATCH. HIS CONDITIONS WERE THAT EACH BOXER MUST RAISE 250 POUNDS FOR THE PRIZE MONEY AND THE MATCH MUST TAKE PLACE WITHIN THREE MONTHS.

MENDOZA REPLIED, AGAIN PUBLICLY, WITH A LETTER CLAIMING THAT HE COULD NOT RAISE THAT MUCH MONEY FROM HIS BACKERS SO QUICKLY. HE ALSO REFERRED TO HIS KIDNEY PROBLEMS, WHICH HIS DOCTOR CONFIRMED IN A SEPARATE LETTER, AND WROTE THAT HE COULD NOT BE SURE HE WOULD BE WELL WITHIN THREE MONTHS.

HUMPHRIES REPLIED AGAIN, DOUBTING MENDOZA'S CLAIMS OF ILL HEALTH AND HINTING THAT THE BOXER WAS AFRAID OF A REMATCH.

MENDOZA WROTE YET AGAIN TO THE PAPERS, THIS TIME OFFERING TO FIGHT HUMPHRIES BY OCTOBER.

LORD STEVENS, DEAR, HAVE YOU HEARD? MENDOZA HAS AGREED TO A REMATCH BY OCTOBER.

"...THE WHOLE TENOR OF HIS LETTER ONLY PROVES THAT PARRYING, NOT FIGHTING, IS THE END OF HIS WISHES."

MORE TAUNTS AND ACCUSATIONS PASSED BACK AND FORTH IN THE PAPERS. IN THIS WAY THE RIVALRY BETWEEN THE TWO BOXERS HAD BECOME AS MUCH OF A STORY AS THE BOXING MATCH.

SIR THOMAS APREECE WAS A WEALTHY PROMOTER OF BOXING AND MENDOZA'S PATRON.

IN MAY 1788, AS SOON AS MENDOZA REGAINED HIS HEALTH, APREECE INVITED MENDOZA TO HIS MANOR HOUSE IN THE COUNTRY TO TRAIN FOR THE NEXT MATCH AGAINST HUMPHRIES.

APREECE WASN'T JUST A BOXING FAN. HE WAS A SERIOUS BOXER, REPUTED TO BE THE MOST SKILLED PUGILIST OF HIS SOCIAL CLASS.

YOU WERE TOO CONFIDENT LAST TIME, DANIEL.

HUMPHRIES TRAINED, AND THAT'S WHY HE WON. THIS TIME YOU'LL TRAIN, AND YOU SHALL BE VICTORIOUS!

HOW...MUCH... FARTHER?

OH, DANIEL, PERHAPS I SHOULD FIGHT HUMPHRIES!

Mr Daniel Mendoza

BUT IN THE MIDST OF HIS TRAINING, AT THE END OF JUNE, MENDOZA RECEIVED TERRIBLE NEWS.

HIS INFANT DAUGHTER SARAH HAD DIED.

יִתְגַּדַּל וְיִתְקַדַּשׁ שְׁמֵהּ רַבָּא*.

* "YITGADAL VE-YITKADASH SHEMEH RABA" MEANS, "MAY HIS GREAT NAME BE SANCTIFIED AND EXALTED."

THE BEREAVED PARENTS MOURNED ACCORDING TO JEWISH CUSTOM. FOR SEVEN DAYS THEY GRIEVED IN THE COMPANY OF RELATIVES AND FRIENDS, AVOIDING COMFORTS SUCH AS CUSHIONS AND RECITING THE KADDISH, A PRAYER TRADITIONALLY OFFERED IN HONOR OF THE DEAD.

BUT AFTER A WEEK IT WAS TIME TO RETURN TO WORK. AND FOR DANIEL MENDOZA, WORK WAS BOXING.

47

DANIEL COMPROMISED WITH ESTHER, WHO WANTED HIM TO GIVE UP BOXING ONCE AND FOR ALL. HE WOULDN'T TRAIN OR BOX IMMEDIATELY, AND HE WOULD CONTINUE TO WEAR BLACK MOURNING CLOTHES, BUT HE WOULD BE PRESENT AT HIS "ACADEMIES" WHERE OTHERS WOULD SPAR UNDER HIS INSTRUCTION.

AND HE LET IT BE KNOWN THAT HE MIGHT POSTPONE THE OCTOBER MATCH.

BUT ALMOST AS SOON AS MENDOZA RETURNED, HUMPHRIES CAME TO PAY A VISIT, AND NOT TO OFFER CONDOLENCES.

THE DATE WAS JULY 5, 1788.

A NEWSPAPER REPORTER ACCOMPANIED THE PARTY. IT IS THANKS TO HIS REPORT THAT WE KNOW WHAT THE TWO RIVALS SAID.

I WANT TO KNOW, MR. MENDOZA, WHETHER YOU WILL FIGHT ME ON THE FIRST OF OCTOBER?

I WISH TO KNOW, THAT I MAY BE CERTAIN AT ONCE, AND NOT BE TOLD, THAT YOU WILL AND YOU WILL NOT.

I AM NOT AT ALL, SIR, IN A CONDITION FOR FIGHTING.

49

53

MENDOZA MADE HIS ACCEPTANCE OF HUMPHRIES'S CHALLENGE OFFICIAL BY WRITING TO THE NEWSPAPERS. BUT HE ADDED A CONDITION: THE MATCH WOULD BE ON GRASS, NOT A STAGE.

I SHALL BE READY TO MEET YOU BY THE FIRST SPRING MEETING AT NEWMARKET, OR ANY OTHER PLACE MUTUALLY TO BE AGREED ON, TO BE DECIDED ON THE TURF.

IN THE EIGHTEENTH CENTURY BOXING WAS NOT COMPLETELY SEPARATED FROM WRESTLING. "PUGILISTS" WERE ALLOWED TO "THROW" THEIR OPPONENTS DOWN, AND HUMPHRIES WAS PARTICULARLY ADEPT AT THROWING. THIS COULD BE ESPECIALLY PAINFUL ON A WOODEN STAGE. MENDOZA THEREFORE PREFERRED TO FIGHT ON GRASS, WHERE THE BLOW OF BEING THROWN WOULD BE CUSHIONED.

I HAVE SEEN YOUR LETTER, AND ACCEPT YOUR CHALLENGE. I AM GLAD YOU HAVE AT LAST FOUND OUT YOUR MIND. THE TERMS SHALL BE SETTLED AT A MEETING, WHICH I WILL APPOINT BY A PRIVATE LETTER TO YOU.

THE BOXERS MET ON AUGUST 6 AT THE CROWN AND MAGPIE PUB IN WHITECHAPEL (MENDOZA'S NEIGHBORHOOD). HUMPHRIES REFUSED TO FIGHT ON TURF AND INSISTED ON OTHER CONDITIONS THAT MENDOZA IN TURN REFUSED.

THE BATTLE OF PUBLIC OPINION GREW MORE HEATED STILL, AS MENDOZA AND HUMPHRIES USED THE NEWSPAPERS TO ACCUSE EACH OTHER OF COWARDICE.

AT LAST THE REMATCH TOOK PLACE.
AFTER NUMEROUS NEGOTIATIONS,
HUMPHRIES AGREED TO FIGHT ON GRASS.
AS USUAL, THE THREAT OF POLICE INTERVENTION
KEPT THE LOCATION A SECRET, AND NEWSPAPERS
FREQUENTLY SPECULATED INCORRECTLY ON THE VENUE.

MEANWHILE, A LARGE AMPHITHEATER
WAS BEING ERECTED IN A MEADOW
OUTSIDE THE HOME OF HENRY THORNTON
NEAR STILTON, 70 MILES FROM LONDON.
IT WAS DESIGNED TO HOLD UP TO
THREE THOUSAND SPECTATORS,
AND MR. LEVERTON, THE ENGINEER
WHO DESIGNED IT, EARNED ONE-EIGHTH
OF THE TICKET SALES.

MENDOZA WROTE:

"Wednesday the 6th of May, 1789, was the day appointed
for deciding this contest: upon which occasion,
the public curiosity was excited in highest degree;
sporting men and amateurs repaired from all
parts of the country, and our amphitheatre was,
in a short space of time, completely filled with spectators,
ardently waiting to see the result of this contest,
and notwithstanding the immense number present,
the most perfect order and regularity prevailed..."

"...with the exception
of one instance —
a Mr. FEWTERELL
who had endeavoured
to gain a sight of the
exhibition, free of expence,
actually climbed over
the inclosure,
though it was furnished
with iron spikes to
prevent such attempts."

"This intrusion
caused some little
disturbance at the time,
but order was
speedily restored."

"Upon this occasion JOHNSON and FORD were
Mr. HUMPHREY'S seconds, and BROWN and RYAN were mine.
Mr. COOMBES and Sir THOMAS A. PRICE (Apreece) were umpires;
the former being nominated on the part of my antagonist,
and the latter chosen by me."

AND SO THE REMATCH BEGAN...

55

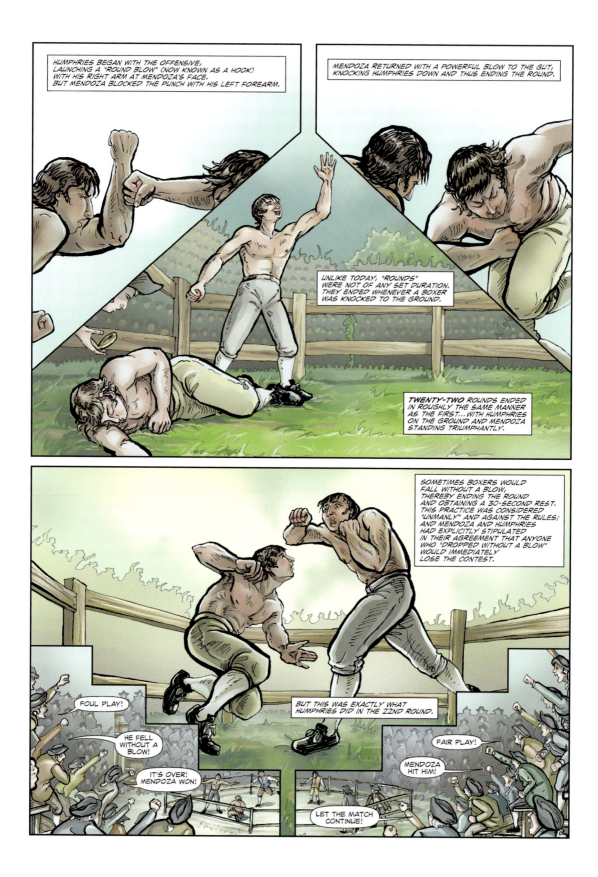

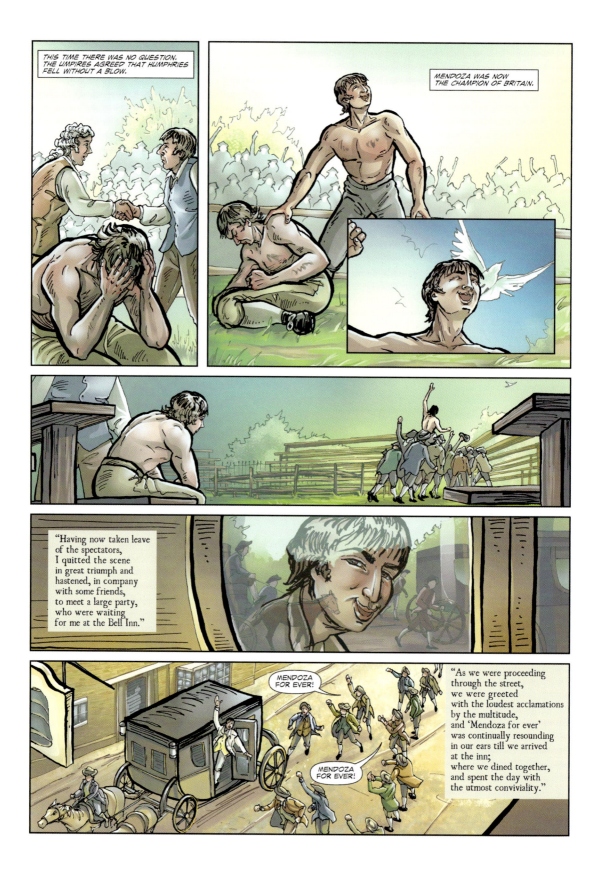

THIS TIME THERE WAS NO QUESTION. THE UMPIRES AGREED THAT HUMPHRIES FELL WITHOUT A BLOW.

MENDOZA WAS NOW THE CHAMPION OF BRITAIN.

"Having now taken leave of the spectators, I quitted the scene in great triumph and hastened, in company with some friends, to meet a large party, who were waiting for me at the Bell Inn."

MENDOZA FOR EVER!

MENDOZA FOR EVER!

"As we were proceeding through the street, we were greeted with the loudest acclamations by the multitude, and 'Mendoza for ever' was continually resounding in our ears till we arrived at the inn; where we dined together, and spent the day with the utmost conviviality."

CHAPTER 5
DONCASTER

MENDOZA EARNED MORE THAN A THOUSAND POUNDS FOR HIS VICTORY AT STILTON.
HE BOUGHT A "COACH AND SIX," A LUXURIOUS CARRIAGE AND SIX FINE HORSES TO PULL IT.
AND OF COURSE HE HIRED A DRIVER.

HE WORE FASHIONABLE CLOTHES, INCLUDING A SUIT THAT A SUPPORTER GAVE HIM.

EVEN HIS BUTTONS SENT A MESSAGE.

HE DIDN'T FORGET ESTHER. HE BOUGHT HER THE LATEST FASHIONS.

YOU DO LIKE THIS DRESS, DON'T YOU ESTHER? I CAN HAVE THE DRESSMAKER SEW YOU A DIFFERENT ONE.

IT'S LOVELY, DAN. I JUST WORRY THAT YOU SPEND YOUR MONEY AS QUICKLY AS YOU EARN IT. WE SHOULD SAVE.

I KNOW, I KNOW. I JUST WANT US TO RISE UP IN SOCIETY.

I WANT PEOPLE TO TREAT ME AS A GENTLEMAN, AND I WANT THEM TO TREAT YOU AS A LADY.

* "BARUCH HA-SHEM" MEANS
"PRAISED BE HIS NAME."

OTHER THINGS WERE HAPPENING IN MAY 1789.
IN FRANCE, KING LOUIS XVI CALLED THE ESTATES GENERAL, A GROUP OF DELEGATES
CHARGED WITH REFORMING THE MONARCHY AND MAKING IT RESPONSIBLE TO THE CITIZENS.

WARREN HASTINGS, THE CHIEF BRITISH COLONIAL OFFICIAL IN INDIA,
WAS CHARGED WITH CORRUPTION AND IMPEACHED
BY MEMBER OF PARLIAMENT EDMUND BURKE.

IN AMERICA, GEORGE WASHINGTON WAS BEGINNING HIS
FIRST TERM AS THE FIRST PRESIDENT OF THE UNITED STATES.

THE NEWSPAPERS REPORTED
THESE MOMENTOUS EVENTS,
AND ORDINARY BRITONS
DISCUSSED THEM.
BUT THE PAPERS ALSO REPORTED
THE RIVALRY BETWEEN MENDOZA
AND HUMPHRIES, WHICH EXCITED
EQUALLY ANIMATED DISCUSSIONS.

IMAGINE THAT!
HUMPHRIES FALLING
WITHOUT A BLOW.

AND TWICE!

IT'S NOT
HARD TO EXPLAIN.
HUMPHRIES FOUGHT
A CROSS!

ARE YOU
SAYING THE
MATCH AT STILTON
WASN'T REAL?

BUT MY NIECE'S
BROTHER-IN-LAW WAS THERE.
HE SAW THE WHOLE THING.
IT WAS REAL.

I'VE ALSO
HEARD THE OUTCOME
WAS PREARRANGED.
HUMPHRIES COULD HAVE
KEPT FIGHTING,
BUT HE HAD BEEN
PAID TO LOSE.

WHY ELSE
WOULD HE
HAVE DROPPED
WITHOUT A
BLOW?

MENDOZA WAS ANGERED BY SUCH RUMORS BUT HE WAS WILLING TO IGNORE THEM. HE WAS NOW THE CHAMPION; AND, BESIDES, HE HAD A BUSINESS TO RUN.

HUMPHRIES WAS LESS PREPARED TO LOOK THE OTHER WAY. HIS BRUISES HADN'T HEALED BEFORE HE WAS DEFENDING HIS CONDUCT AND CHALLENGING MENDOZA TO A FINAL CONTEST.

HE MADE THE NOVEL STIPULATION THAT NO MONEY BE COLLECTED FROM THE SPECTATORS. THUS THE FIGHT WOULD BE FOR HONOR, NOT MONEY.

YOU DON'T HAVE TO SAY ANYTHING.

I WON'T FIGHT.

MENDOZA IGNORED HUMPHRIES'S CHALLENGE AND INSTEAD EMBARKED ON MORE PEACEABLE VENTURES. HE OPENED A NEW "ACADEMY" IN THE FAMOUS LYCEUM THEATRE TO ACCOMMODATE HIS GROWING POPULARITY.

LADIES AND GENTLEMEN, ALLOW ME TO DISPLAY OUR NATIONAL SPORT...

TO EXPAND HIS APPEAL TO MIDDLE- AND UPPER-CLASS WOMEN; AND TO PLACATE THE AUTHORITIES WHO WERE CONCERNED ABOUT VIOLENT DISPLAYS IN PUBLIC PLACES, HE ELIMINATED PHYSICAL CONTACT FROM HIS EXHIBITION.

REALLY, IT'S LESS BRUTAL THAN FENCING.

THERE'S NO REASON WHY WE SHOULDN'T BE HERE.

THEATRE ROYAL

LYCEUM

MENDOZA COULD ALSO BE SEEN AT THE ROYAL CIRCUS, A POPULAR COVERED AMPHITHEATER THAT FEATURED VARIETY SHOWS. THERE HE ENGAGED IN A "PANTOMIME" SPARRING MATCH WITH THE IRISH BOXER RYAN.

ANOTHER POPULAR ACT IN THE VARIETY SHOW WAS A REENACTMENT OF THE STORMING OF THE BASTILLE PRISON, AN EVENT THAT HAD OCCURRED ONLY WEEKS EARLIER AT THE OUTSET OF THE FRENCH REVOLUTION.

LET US ATTACK AND I WILL LEAD THE CHARGE!

PERHAPS THE FRENCH WILL BE A FREE NATION TOO.

MAYBE IRELAND WILL BE NEXT.

WHEN MENDOZA TRAVELED ANYWHERE, HE WAS GREETED BY ADMIRING CROWDS. ONCE, WHEN TRAVELING WITH THOMAS APREECE TO PETERBOROUGH, 70 MILES FROM LONDON:

"The inhabitants, having, by some means, gained information of my being in the chaise, surrounded us, on our entrance in the town, in such numbers, that we were actually prevented from proceeding on our journey, till after SIR THOMAS had addressed them, and proposed that in order to gratify their curiosity..."

"...we should stand for some time on one of the benches in the market place, and we were accordingly compelled to stand there upwards of an hour, bowing and paying our respects to the populace, till at length they began to disperse, and we were enabled to proceed to the end of our journey."

MENDOZA WAS RICH. HE WAS FAMOUS. HE HAD A LOVING WIFE AND WOULD SOON BE A FATHER. HE HAD REASON TO CONSIDER HIMSELF FULFILLED. BUT THE CHALLENGES FROM HUMPHRIES KEPT COMING, AND MENDOZA FELT AN OVERWHELMING DESIRE TO FIGHT.

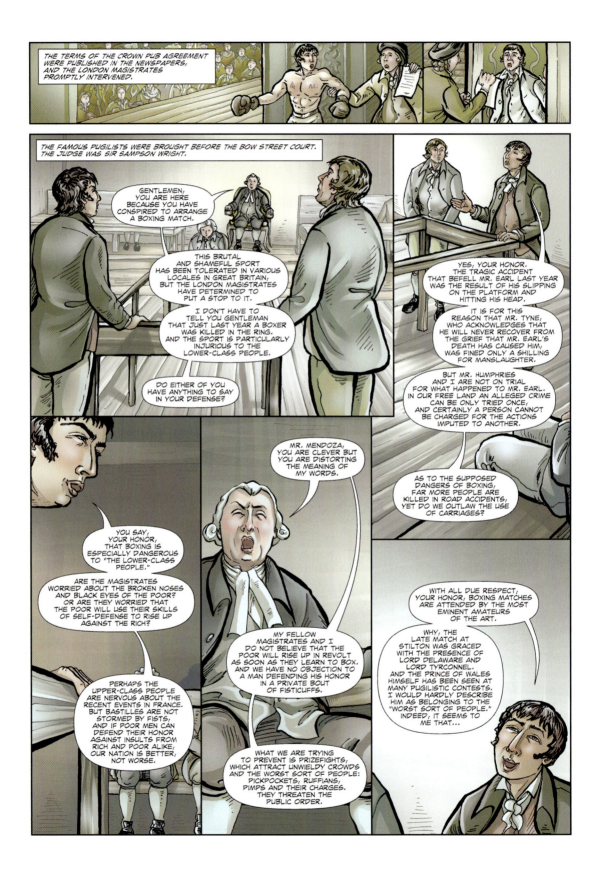

THE TERMS OF THE CROWN PUB AGREEMENT WERE PUBLISHED IN THE NEWSPAPERS, AND THE LONDON MAGISTRATES PROMPTLY INTERVENED.

THE FAMOUS PUGILISTS WERE BROUGHT BEFORE THE BOW STREET COURT. THE JUDGE WAS SIR SAMPSON WRIGHT.

GENTLEMEN, YOU ARE HERE BECAUSE YOU HAVE CONSPIRED TO ARRANGE A BOXING MATCH.

THIS BRUTAL AND SHAMEFUL SPORT HAS BEEN TOLERATED IN VARIOUS LOCALES IN GREAT BRITAIN, BUT THE LONDON MAGISTRATES HAVE DETERMINED TO PUT A STOP TO IT.

I DON'T HAVE TO TELL YOU GENTLEMAN THAT JUST LAST YEAR A BOXER WAS KILLED IN THE RING, AND THE SPORT IS PARTICULARLY INJURIOUS TO THE LOWER-CLASS PEOPLE.

DO EITHER OF YOU HAVE ANYTHING TO SAY IN YOUR DEFENSE?

YES, YOUR HONOR. THE TRAGIC ACCIDENT THAT BEFELL MR. EARL LAST YEAR WAS THE RESULT OF HIS SLIPPING ON THE PLATFORM AND HITTING HIS HEAD.

IT IS FOR THIS REASON THAT MR. TYNE, WHO ACKNOWLEDGES THAT HE WILL NEVER RECOVER FROM THE GRIEF THAT MR. EARL'S DEATH HAS CAUSED HIM, WAS FINED ONLY A SHILLING FOR MANSLAUGHTER.

BUT MR. HUMPHRIES AND I ARE NOT ON TRIAL FOR WHAT HAPPENED TO MR. EARL. IN OUR FREE LAND AN ALLEGED CRIME CAN BE ONLY TRIED ONCE, AND CERTAINLY A PERSON CANNOT BE CHARGED FOR THE ACTIONS IMPUTED TO ANOTHER.

AS TO THE SUPPOSED DANGERS OF BOXING, FAR MORE PEOPLE ARE KILLED IN ROAD ACCIDENTS, YET DO WE OUTLAW THE USE OF CARRIAGES?

MR. MENDOZA, YOU ARE CLEVER BUT YOU ARE DISTORTING THE MEANING OF MY WORDS.

YOU SAY, YOUR HONOR, THAT BOXING IS ESPECIALLY DANGEROUS TO "THE LOWER-CLASS PEOPLE."

ARE THE MAGISTRATES WORRIED ABOUT THE BROKEN NOSES AND BLACK EYES OF THE POOR? OR ARE THEY WORRIED THAT THE POOR WILL USE THEIR SKILLS OF SELF-DEFENSE TO RISE UP AGAINST THE RICH?

PERHAPS THE UPPER-CLASS PEOPLE ARE NERVOUS ABOUT THE RECENT EVENTS IN FRANCE. BUT BASTILLES ARE NOT STORMED BY FISTS, AND IF POOR MEN CAN DEFEND THEIR HONOR AGAINST INSULTS FROM RICH AND POOR ALIKE, OUR NATION IS BETTER, NOT WORSE.

MY FELLOW MAGISTRATES AND I DO NOT BELIEVE THAT THE POOR WILL RISE UP IN REVOLT AS SOON AS THEY LEARN TO BOX. AND WE HAVE NO OBJECTION TO A MAN DEFENDING HIS HONOR IN A PRIVATE BOUT OF FISTICUFFS.

WHAT WE ARE TRYING TO PREVENT IS PRIZEFIGHTS, WHICH ATTRACT UNWIELDY CROWDS AND THE WORST SORT OF PEOPLE: PICKPOCKETS, RUFFIANS, PIMPS AND THEIR CHARGES. THEY THREATEN THE PUBLIC ORDER.

WITH ALL DUE RESPECT, YOUR HONOR, BOXING MATCHES ARE ATTENDED BY THE MOST EMINENT AMATEURS OF THE ART.

WHY, THE LATE MATCH AT STILTON WAS GRACED WITH THE PRESENCE OF LORD DELAWARE AND LORD TYRCONNEL, AND THE PRINCE OF WALES HIMSELF HAS BEEN SEEN AT MANY PUGILISTIC CONTESTS. I WOULD HARDLY DESCRIBE HIM AS BELONGING TO THE "WORST SORT OF PEOPLE." INDEED, IT SEEMS TO ME THAT...

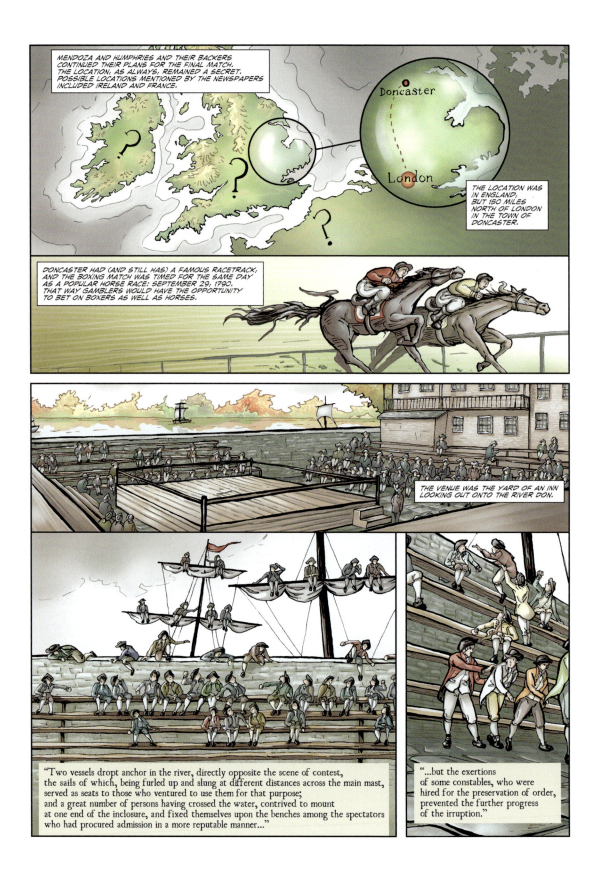

MENDOZA AND HUMPHRIES AND THEIR BACKERS CONTINUED THEIR PLANS FOR THE FINAL MATCH. THE LOCATION, AS ALWAYS, REMAINED A SECRET. POSSIBLE LOCATIONS MENTIONED BY THE NEWSPAPERS INCLUDED IRELAND AND FRANCE.

Doncaster

London

THE LOCATION WAS IN ENGLAND, BUT 150 MILES NORTH OF LONDON IN THE TOWN OF DONCASTER.

DONCASTER HAD (AND STILL HAS) A FAMOUS RACETRACK, AND THE BOXING MATCH WAS TIMED FOR THE SAME DAY AS A POPULAR HORSE RACE: SEPTEMBER 29, 1790. THAT WAY GAMBLERS WOULD HAVE THE OPPORTUNITY TO BET ON BOXERS AS WELL AS HORSES.

THE VENUE WAS THE YARD OF AN INN LOOKING OUT ONTO THE RIVER DON.

"Two vessels dropt anchor in the river, directly opposite the scene of contest, the sails of which, being furled up and slung at different distances across the main mast, served as seats to those who ventured to use them for that purpose; and a great number of persons having crossed the water, contrived to mount at one end of the inclosure, and fixed themselves upon the benches among the spectators who had procured admission in a more reputable manner..."

"...but the exertions of some constables, who were hired for the preservation of order, prevented the further progress of the irruption."

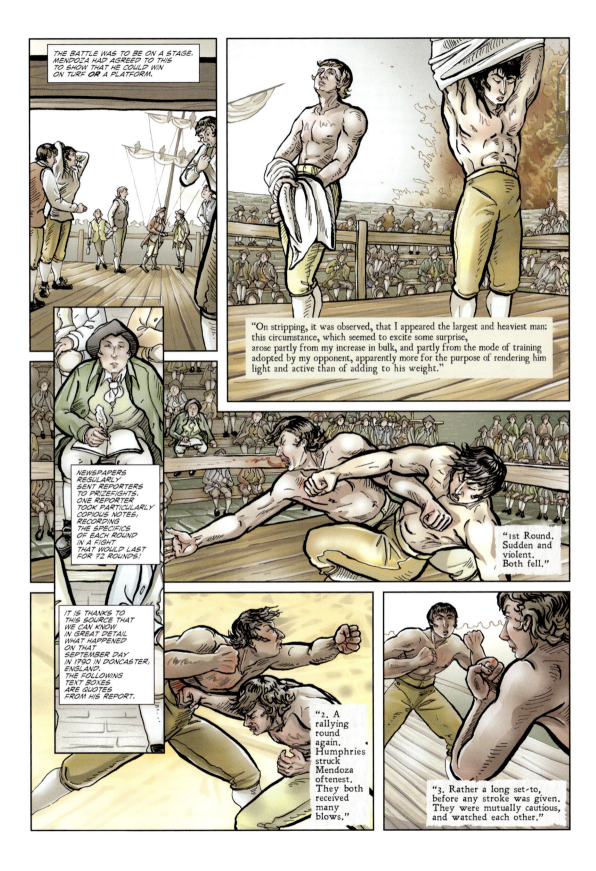

THE BATTLE WAS TO BE ON A STAGE. MENDOZA HAD AGREED TO THIS TO SHOW THAT HE COULD WIN ON TURF **OR** A PLATFORM.

"On stripping, it was observed, that I appeared the largest and heaviest man: this circumstance, which seemed to excite some surprise, arose partly from my increase in bulk, and partly from the mode of training adopted by my opponent, apparently more for the purpose of rendering him light and active than of adding to his weight."

NEWSPAPERS REGULARLY SENT REPORTERS TO PRIZEFIGHTS. ONE REPORTER TOOK PARTICULARLY COPIOUS NOTES, RECORDING THE SPECIFICS OF EACH ROUND IN A FIGHT THAT WOULD LAST FOR 72 ROUNDS!

"1st Round. Sudden and violent. Both fell."

IT IS THANKS TO THIS SOURCE THAT WE CAN KNOW IN GREAT DETAIL WHAT HAPPENED ON THAT SEPTEMBER DAY IN 1790 IN DONCASTER, ENGLAND. THE FOLLOWING TEXT BOXES ARE QUOTES FROM HIS REPORT.

"2. A rallying round again. Humphries struck Mendoza oftenest. They both received many blows."

"3. Rather a long set-to, before any stroke was given. They were mutually cautious, and watched each other."

"17. Humphries aimed at the face. Mendoza stopped, and was about to return, when Humphries fell. (Cry of 'foul, foul!' in consequence of Humphries' dropping without a blow: succeeded by a cry of 'fair, fair!')."

"18. Mendoza aimed at Humphries' face. Humphries fell without a blow."

"20. Mendoza struck Humphries in the face. Seemed to forget that he was not sparring, and hit him twice open-handed. Humphries fell."

"31. Short round. Humphries struck Mendoza, and cut him near the right temple. Mendoza struck again, and Humphries fell."

"48. Hits on both sides. Humphries closing, attempted to fall. Mendoza prevented him, by holding him round the neck with the left hand, and lifting his right in the air for some moments..."

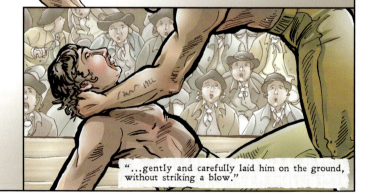

"...gently and carefully laid him on the ground, without striking a blow."

MENDOZA IS TOYING WITH HIM. HE HASN'T COMPLAINED ABOUT HUMPHRIES'S FALLING WITHOUT A BLOW; AND JUST THEN HE COULD HAVE ENDED THE MATCH.

YES, IT'S AS IF PLAYING FAIR ISN'T ENOUGH FOR HIM. HE HAS TO BE *MORE* THAN FAIR.

"51. Mendoza sprung forward, and struck a strait blow over Humphries's mouth. Sprung forward again, and repeated the stroke. Humphries was much cut between the nose and upper lip."

"52. Mendoza struck strait forward, and cut Humphries over the nose. Humphries bled much, and aimed a returning blow. Mendoza stopped it, springing forward, cut him on the left eye, and Humphries fell."

"61. Humphries struck. Mendoza returned. Closed. Humphries was falling. Mendoza held him up, and for a few moments remained with his right hand uplifted; when instead of taking advantage of his situation, he lowered him carefully to the ground."

HE'S DONE IT AGAIN!

I DON'T UNDERSTAND. HE COULD HAVE ENDED THE MATCH AGAIN.

IT'S NOT SURPRISING. IF MENDOZA HAD HIT HIM, THE CHRISTIANS WOULD HAVE SAID HUMPHRIES WAS "DOWN" EVEN THOUGH HE WAS DROPPING WITHOUT A BLOW. THEY WOULD HAVE CRIED "FOUL!" AND SAID THE JEW WAS CHEATING.

IT'S NOT ENOUGH FOR US JEWS TO BE HONEST. WE HAVE TO BE BETTER THAN THE CHRISTIANS JUST TO AVOID BEING ACCUSED OF DISHONESTY.

"68. Humphries attempted to strike. Mendoza stopped the blow, and hit him in the eye; so that the blood gushed forth, and Humphries fell."

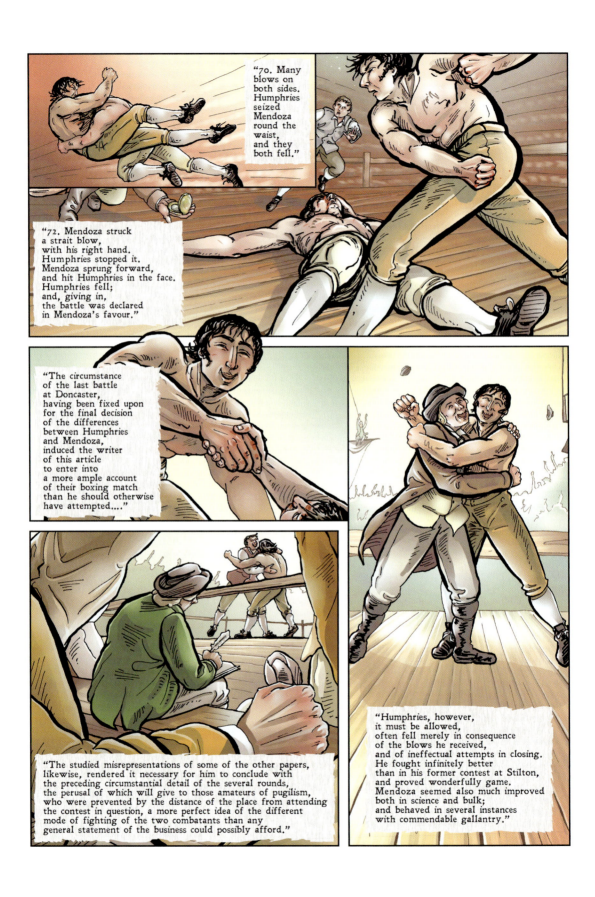

"70. Many blows on both sides. Humphries seized Mendoza round the waist, and they both fell."

"72. Mendoza struck a strait blow, with his right hand. Humphries stopped it. Mendoza sprung forward, and hit Humphries in the face. Humphries fell; and, giving in, the battle was declared in Mendoza's favour."

"The circumstance of the last battle at Doncaster, having been fixed upon for the final decision of the differences between Humphries and Mendoza, induced the writer of this article to enter into a more ample account of their boxing match than he should otherwise have attempted...."

"The studied misrepresentations of some of the other papers, likewise, rendered it necessary for him to conclude with the preceding circumstantial detail of the several rounds, the perusal of which will give to those amateurs of pugilism, who were prevented by the distance of the place from attending the contest in question, a more perfect idea of the different mode of fighting of the two combatants than any general statement of the business could possibly afford."

"Humphries, however, it must be allowed, often fell merely in consequence of the blows he received, and of ineffectual attempts in closing. He fought infinitely better than in his former contest at Stilton, and proved wonderfully game. Mendoza seemed also much improved both in science and bulk; and behaved in several instances with commendable gallantry."

"Having said thus much
we shall press the business
no longer upon
the public attention,
but conclude by
repeating our wish,
that as the friends
of Humphries
during the last battle
admired the spirit
of the Jew,
and those of Mendoza
praised the perseverance
and bottom of the Christian,
and as those pugilists have
decided their final contest,
and done all that can
be expected from them
as enemies, they may,
for the sake of novelty,
try the effects
of a firm and
lasting friendship."

CHAPTER 6
"POOR DAN MENDOZA"

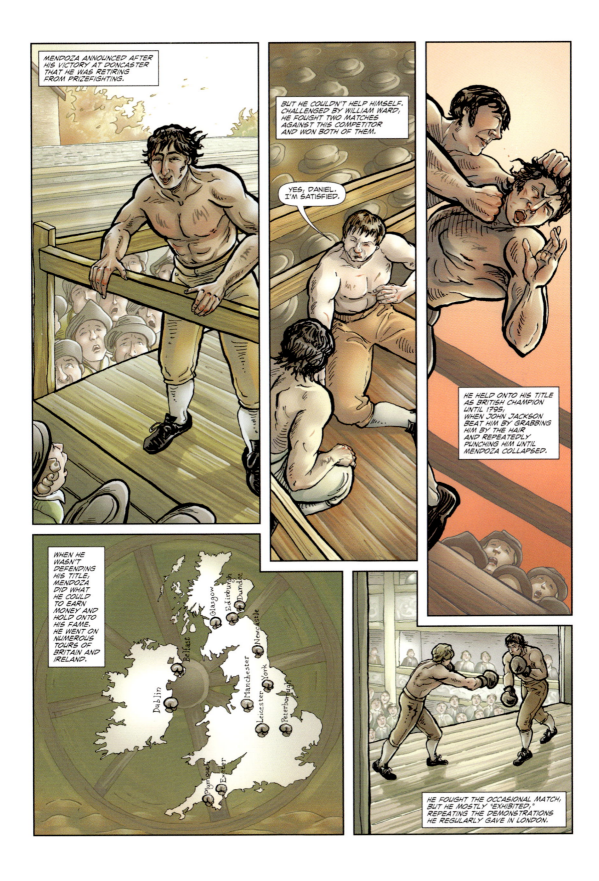

MENDOZA ANNOUNCED AFTER HIS VICTORY AT DONCASTER THAT HE WAS RETIRING FROM PRIZEFIGHTING.

BUT HE COULDN'T HELP HIMSELF. CHALLENGED BY WILLIAM WARD, HE FOUGHT TWO MATCHES AGAINST THIS COMPETITOR AND WON BOTH OF THEM.

YES, DANIEL. I'M SATISFIED.

HE HELD ONTO HIS TITLE AS BRITISH CHAMPION UNTIL 1795, WHEN JOHN JACKSON BEAT HIM BY GRABBING HIM BY THE HAIR AND REPEATEDLY PUNCHING HIM UNTIL MENDOZA COLLAPSED.

WHEN HE WASN'T DEFENDING HIS TITLE, MENDOZA DID WHAT HE COULD TO EARN MONEY AND HOLD ONTO HIS FAME. HE WENT ON NUMEROUS TOURS OF BRITAIN AND IRELAND.

Glasgow
Edinburgh
Dundee
Belfast
Newcastle
Dublin
Manchester
York
Leicester
Peterborough
Plymouth
Exeter

HE FOUGHT THE OCCASIONAL MATCH, BUT HE MOSTLY "EXHIBITED," REPEATING THE DEMONSTRATIONS HE REGULARLY GAVE IN LONDON.

HIS FAME WAS SUCH THAT EVEN THE KING TOOK NOTICE.
THOUGH THE PRINCE OF WALES PUBLICLY DISAVOWED BOXING AND THE KING NEVER SPOKE OFFICIALLY OF IT, IN PRIVATE THEY BELIEVED IT TO BE THE "MANLY" AND "BRITISH" SPORT ITS FANS CLAIMED IT TO BE.

"...I went for a few days to Windsor, and, during my stay in that town, had the honour of being introduced to a great personage. This happened, one evening on the terrace, where I was walking, and was suddenly surprised at being accosted by a nobleman, who, in a very abrupt manner, mentioned his intention of introducing me to his m—y."

"He had scarcely spoken when the king, attended by some lords in waiting, approached the spot, upon which, I was introduced, and had the honour of a long conversation with his m—y, who made many ingenious remarks on the pugilistic art, such as might naturally be expected to be made by a person of so comprehensive a mind and such transcendent abilities, as that illustrious personage is generally believed to possess!"

"Before I quitted the terrace, the princess royal (now queen of Wirtemberg) brought one of the younger branches of the royal family to me, and asked my permission (which I of course readily granted) for this young gentleman to strike me a blow, in order that he might have to boast at a subsequent opportunity of having at an early period of his life, struck a professed pugilist on Windsor terrace."

BUT FAME DID NOT SAVE MENDOZA FROM TROUBLES WITH THE LAW. IN OCTOBER 1793 HE WAS CHARGED WITH RECEIVING STOLEN GOODS.

HE WAS ACQUITTED, BUT HE WOULD FIND HIMSELF IN COURT AGAIN.

HOUNDED BY CREDITORS, HE TURNED HIMSELF IN AND WAS FOUND GUILTY OF NEGLECTING TO REPAY NUMEROUS DEBTS.

HE BECAME A PRISONER "WITHIN THE RULES OF THE KING'S BENCH," WHICH MEANT HE DID NOT HAVE TO BE CONFINED TO PRISON, BUT HE HAD TO LIVE AND WORK IN THE NEIGHBORHOOD SURROUNDING THE PRISON UNTIL HE PAID HIS DEBTS. HE OPENED A SHOP SELLING OIL AND CANDLES, AND THOUGH THIS BUSINESS FAILED, HE SOMEHOW MANAGED TO PAY ENOUGH OF HIS DEBTS TO BE FREED.

HIS MANY TOURS SUSTAINED HIS FAME AND PROVIDED HIM WITH INCOME, BUT THEY ALSO ALLOWED HIM TO STAY ONE STEP AHEAD OF HIS CREDITORS.

BUT IN 1799 THE LAW CAUGHT UP WITH HIM IN CARLISLE IN THE NORTH OF ENGLAND, AND HE SPENT SIX MONTHS IN THE CARLISLE PRISON.

UPON HIS RELEASE, HE TOURED MANY TOWNS AND CITIES, EXHIBITING AND SPARRING WHEREVER HE COULD DRAW A CROWD. BUT HE NO LONGER HAD A FANCY CARRIAGE, AND FOR PART OF HIS LONG JOURNEY BACK TO LONDON HE HAD TO WALK.

HE LONGED TO SEE ESTHER AGAIN, AND THEIR CHILDREN. BUT HE WASN'T PREPARED FOR WHAT HE WOULD SEE WHEN HE WALKED THROUGH THE DOOR.

"On my arrival in London
I found my family in great distress;
an execution had been put in my house,
and it had been stripped
of almost every article of furniture."

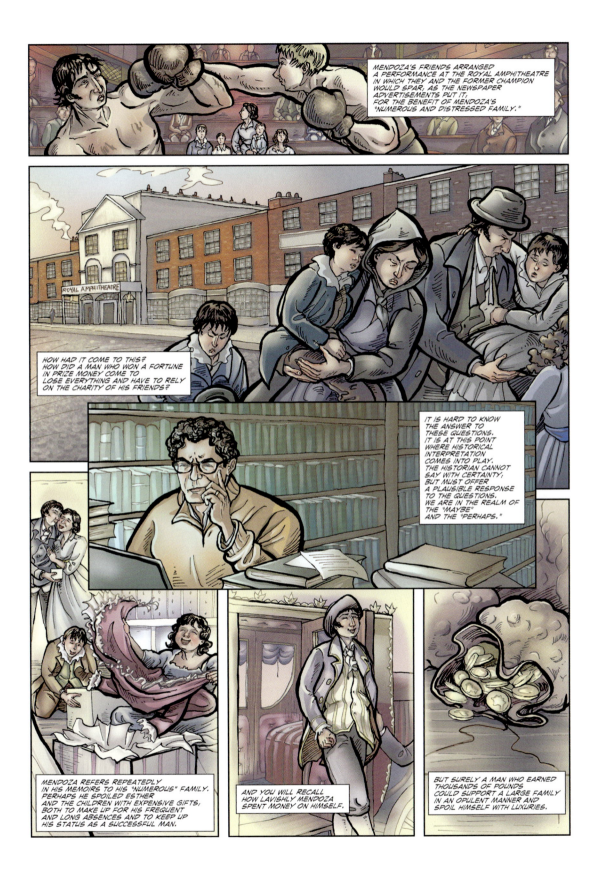

MENDOZA'S FRIENDS ARRANGED A PERFORMANCE AT THE ROYAL AMPHITHEATRE IN WHICH THEY AND THE FORMER CHAMPION WOULD SPAR, AS THE NEWSPAPER ADVERTISEMENTS PUT IT, FOR THE BENEFIT OF MENDOZA'S "NUMEROUS AND DISTRESSED FAMILY."

HOW HAD IT COME TO THIS? HOW DID A MAN WHO WON A FORTUNE IN PRIZE MONEY COME TO LOSE EVERYTHING AND HAVE TO RELY ON THE CHARITY OF HIS FRIENDS?

IT IS HARD TO KNOW THE ANSWER TO THESE QUESTIONS. IT IS AT THIS POINT WHERE HISTORICAL INTERPRETATION COMES INTO PLAY. THE HISTORIAN CANNOT SAY WITH CERTAINTY; BUT MUST OFFER A PLAUSIBLE RESPONSE TO THE QUESTIONS. WE ARE IN THE REALM OF THE "MAYBE" AND THE "PERHAPS."

MENDOZA REFERS REPEATEDLY IN HIS MEMOIRS TO HIS "NUMEROUS" FAMILY. PERHAPS HE SPOILED ESTHER AND THE CHILDREN WITH EXPENSIVE GIFTS, BOTH TO MAKE UP FOR HIS FREQUENT AND LONG ABSENCES AND TO KEEP UP HIS STATUS AS A SUCCESSFUL MAN.

AND YOU WILL RECALL HOW LAVISHLY MENDOZA SPENT MONEY ON HIMSELF.

BUT SURELY A MAN WHO EARNED THOUSANDS OF POUNDS COULD SUPPORT A LARGE FAMILY IN AN OPULENT MANNER AND SPOIL HIMSELF WITH LUXURIES.

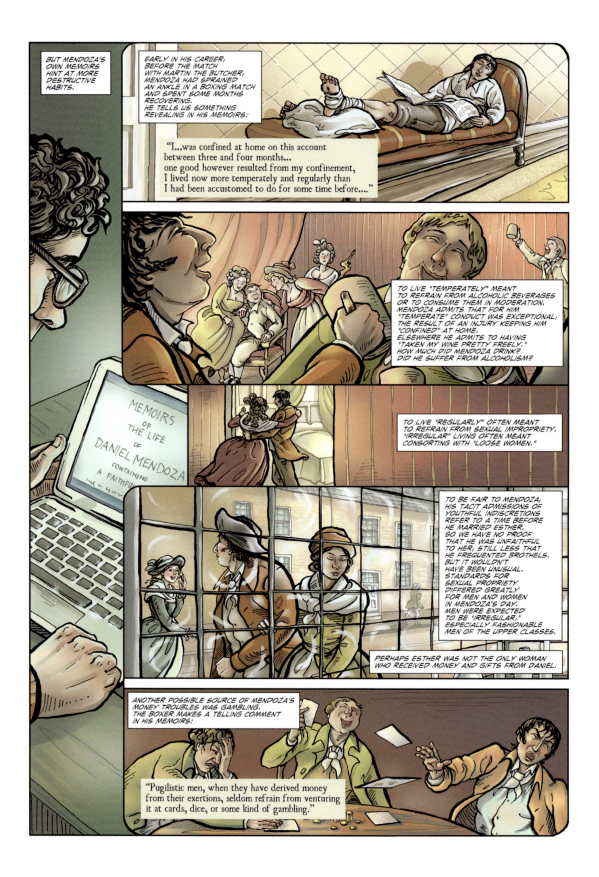

BUT MENDOZA'S OWN MEMOIRS HINT AT MORE DESTRUCTIVE HABITS.

EARLY IN HIS CAREER, BEFORE THE MATCH WITH MARTIN THE BUTCHER, MENDOZA HAD SPRAINED AN ANKLE IN A BOXING MATCH AND SPENT SOME MONTHS RECOVERING.
HE TELLS US SOMETHING REVEALING IN HIS MEMOIRS:

"I...was confined at home on this account between three and four months... one good however resulted from my confinement, I lived now more temperately and regularly than I had been accustomed to do for some time before...."

TO LIVE "TEMPERATELY" MEANT TO REFRAIN FROM ALCOHOLIC BEVERAGES OR TO CONSUME THEM IN MODERATION. MENDOZA ADMITS THAT FOR HIM "TEMPERATE" CONDUCT WAS EXCEPTIONAL; THE RESULT OF AN INJURY KEEPING HIM "CONFINED" AT HOME.
ELSEWHERE HE ADMITS TO HAVING "TAKEN MY WINE PRETTY FREELY."
HOW MUCH DID MENDOZA DRINK? DID HE SUFFER FROM ALCOHOLISM?

TO LIVE "REGULARLY" OFTEN MEANT TO REFRAIN FROM SEXUAL IMPROPRIETY. "IRREGULAR" LIVING OFTEN MEANT CONSORTING WITH "LOOSE WOMEN."

TO BE FAIR TO MENDOZA, HIS TACIT ADMISSIONS OF YOUTHFUL INDISCRETIONS REFER TO A TIME BEFORE HE MARRIED ESTHER.
SO WE HAVE NO PROOF THAT HE WAS UNFAITHFUL TO HER, STILL LESS THAT HE FREQUENTED BROTHELS.
BUT IT WOULDN'T HAVE BEEN UNUSUAL. STANDARDS FOR SEXUAL PROPRIETY DIFFERED GREATLY FOR MEN AND WOMEN IN MENDOZA'S DAY. MEN WERE EXPECTED TO BE "IRREGULAR," ESPECIALLY FASHIONABLE MEN OF THE UPPER CLASSES.

PERHAPS ESTHER WAS NOT THE ONLY WOMAN WHO RECEIVED MONEY AND GIFTS FROM DANIEL.

ANOTHER POSSIBLE SOURCE OF MENDOZA'S MONEY TROUBLES WAS GAMBLING.
THE BOXER MAKES A TELLING COMMENT IN HIS MEMOIRS:

"Pugilistic men, when they have derived money from their exertions, seldom refrain from venturing it at cards, dice, or some kind of gambling."

MEMOIRS OF THE LIFE OF DANIEL MENDOZA CONTAINING A FAITHFUL

THIS WOULDN'T BE SURPRISING.
BOXING AS A SPORT DEPENDED ON GAMBLING, AND MATCHES WERE OFTEN SCHEDULED CLOSE TO THE TIME OF HORSE RACES, ANOTHER OCCASION FOR GAMBLING. CONTEMPORARY NEWSPAPERS CONTAINED MANY REPORTS OF BOXERS APPEARING AT HORSE RACES, AND MENDOZA WAS REPORTED TO HAVE GONE STRAIGHT TO THE DONCASTER RACES AFTER HIS FINAL VICTORY OVER HUMPHRIES. PERHAPS HE HAD A GAMBLING PROBLEM AND LOST MUCH OF HIS FORTUNE IN THIS WAY.

BUT MENDOZA ALSO WORKED AS HARD AS HE PLAYED, AND AS IN HIS YOUTH HE HAD A SERIES OF JOBS. WHILE ON TOUR GIVING PUGILISTIC EXHIBITIONS, HE JOINED UP WITH A TROUPE OF ACTORS AND TRIED TO CULTIVATE HIS THEATRICAL TALENTS.

THEY TURNED OUT TO BE LIMITED.

GO BACK TO BOXING, DANIEL!

IN A TWIST OF FATE, MENDOZA BECAME A SHERIFF'S DEPUTY, AND INSTEAD OF BEING ARRESTED HIMSELF, HE ARRESTED PEOPLE. BUT:

"...my profession sometimes appeared to be of that odious nature, that no pecuniary gains could make amends for the scenes of distress at which it was frequently my task to be present. For instance, what gain...could make amends to a person possessing any feelings of humanity for being sometimes obliged to tear the husband from the wife, or the father from his children, or to seize with unrelenting hand the small stock of furniture, nay, perhaps the only bed of a worthy but unfortunate family, and thereby reduce them to beggary and wretchedness...."

MENDOZA KNEW WHAT IT FELT LIKE TO BE ON THE OTHER SIDE OF THE DOOR.

MENDOZA ALSO HAD A BRIEF PERIOD OF EMPLOYMENT IN THE ARMY, AND HE BECAME A SERGEANT MAJOR IN THE ABERDEEN FENCIBLES. HIS PRINCIPAL JOB WAS AS A "CRIMPER," OR RECRUITER WHO OFTEN USED UNSCRUPULOUS METHODS OF INDUCING YOUNG MEN TO SIGN UP FOR MILITARY SERVICE.

IN 1801 HE SCRAPED TOGETHER ENOUGH MONEY TO OPEN A PUB, WHICH HE PATRIOTICALLY TITLED THE LORD NELSON. ADMIRAL NELSON, WHO WAS DESTINED TO LOSE HIS LIFE IN 1805 WHILE DEFEATING NAPOLEON'S FLEET AT THE BATTLE OF TRAFALGAR, WAS ALREADY A BRITISH HERO FOR HAVING DEFEATED NAPOLEON IN EGYPT IN 1798.

MENDOZA ALSO WORKED FOR A TIME AS A SUTLER, OR TRAVELING PEDDLER TO SOLDIERS AT GARRISONS.

BUT THE PUB FAILED AND MENDOZA WENT BANKRUPT IN 1804. BY THEN, AT LEAST, A NEW LAW PROTECTED INSOLVENT PEOPLE FROM HAVING TO BE INCARCERATED.

IN 1806, AT THE AGE OF 41, MENDOZA WAS SO DESPERATE THAT HE FOUGHT IN ANOTHER PRIZEFIGHT. HIS OPPONENT WAS THE EQUALLY IMPECUNIOUS HARRY LEE, WHO WAS EVEN SEVERAL YEARS OLDER THAN MENDOZA. THE TWO VETERANS BATTLED FOR 50 GUINEAS AND THE "DOOR MONEY," WHICH WAS PROBABLY SUBSTANTIAL, AS THE NEWSPAPERS REPORTED A LARGE CROWD.

MENDOZA WON IN 53 ROUNDS. IT WAS HIS FINAL PRIZEFIGHT.

IN 1809 SPECTATORS PROTESTED RAISED TICKET PRICES AT THE COVENT GARDEN THEATER, INTERRUPTING PERFORMANCES WITH DEMANDS FOR THE "OLD PRICES." THE THEATER MANAGER HIRED MENDOZA AND OTHER FAMOUS "BRUISERS" TO INTIMIDATE AND EVEN BEAT THE PROTESTERS.

MEANWHILE, HIS FAMILY KEPT GROWING. BY 1810 ESTHER AND DANIEL HAD NINE CHILDREN.

MENDOZA RELIED INCREASINGLY ON THE CHARITY OF FRIENDS AND FANS. ACCORDING TO THE NEWSPAPERS HE HAD BENEFIT SPARRING MATCHES IN 1811, 1814, 1817, 1818, 1820, 1822, 1824, 1825, 1827, AND 1829.

BY THE LATE 1820S THE FORMER CHAMPION COULD NO LONGER SPAR, BUT HIS FRIENDS CONTINUED TO HOLD BENEFITS FOR HIM IN WHICH YOUNGER BOXERS PERFORMED. BUT FEWER AND FEWER SEATS WERE FILLED, AND EVENTUALLY THE CHARITY EVENTS STOPPED ALTOGETHER.

MENDOZA DIED ON SEPTEMBER 3, 1836. THE NEWSPAPERS, WHICH HAD ONCE BEEN FILLED WITH HIS EXPLOITS, HAD LITTLE TO SAY ABOUT THE NOW LARGELY FORGOTTEN FIGHTER. THEY EVEN HAD TO EXPLAIN THAT HE HAD ONCE BEEN A BOXER. THE **MORNING POST** WAS REPRESENTATIVE IN ITS TERSENESS: "ON SATURDAY MORNING, DAN MENDOZA, THE WELL-KNOWN PUGILIST, DIED, AFTER A LONG AND PAINFUL ILLNESS, IN HORSE-SHOE-ALLEY, PETTICOAT-LANE. HE HAD REACHED HIS 73D YEAR, AND RETAINED HIS FACULTIES TO THE LAST. HE HAS LEFT A WIDOW TO DEPLORE HIS LOSS."

IT SEEMS POOR DAN MENDOZA HAS DIED.

REALLY? I DIDN'T KNOW HE WAS STILL ALIVE.

CHAPTER 7
SO WHAT?

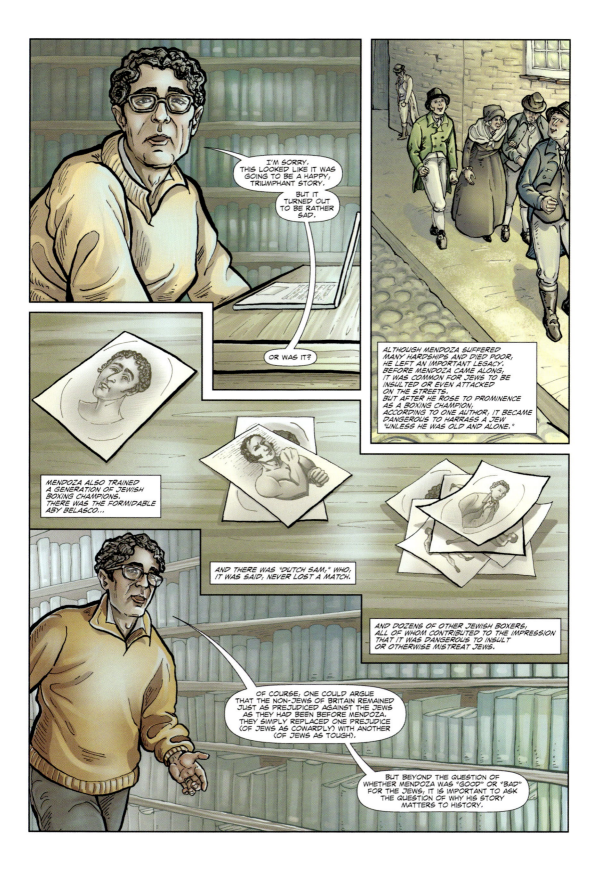

I'M SORRY. THIS LOOKED LIKE IT WAS GOING TO BE A HAPPY, TRIUMPHANT STORY.

BUT IT TURNED OUT TO BE RATHER SAD.

OR WAS IT?

ALTHOUGH MENDOZA SUFFERED MANY HARDSHIPS AND DIED POOR, HE LEFT AN IMPORTANT LEGACY. BEFORE MENDOZA CAME ALONG, IT WAS COMMON FOR JEWS TO BE INSULTED OR EVEN ATTACKED ON THE STREETS. BUT AFTER HE ROSE TO PROMINENCE AS A BOXING CHAMPION, ACCORDING TO ONE AUTHOR, IT BECAME DANGEROUS TO HARRASS A JEW "UNLESS HE WAS OLD AND ALONE."

MENDOZA ALSO TRAINED A GENERATION OF JEWISH BOXING CHAMPIONS. THERE WAS THE FORMIDABLE ABY BELASCO...

AND THERE WAS "DUTCH SAM," WHO, IT WAS SAID, NEVER LOST A MATCH.

AND DOZENS OF OTHER JEWISH BOXERS, ALL OF WHOM CONTRIBUTED TO THE IMPRESSION THAT IT WAS DANGEROUS TO INSULT OR OTHERWISE MISTREAT JEWS.

OF COURSE, ONE COULD ARGUE THAT THE NON-JEWS OF BRITAIN REMAINED JUST AS PREJUDICED AGAINST THE JEWS AS THEY HAD BEEN BEFORE MENDOZA. THEY SIMPLY REPLACED ONE PREJUDICE (OF JEWS AS COWARDLY) WITH ANOTHER (OF JEWS AS TOUGH).

BUT BEYOND THE QUESTION OF WHETHER MENDOZA WAS "GOOD" OR "BAD" FOR THE JEWS, IT IS IMPORTANT TO ASK THE QUESTION OF WHY HIS STORY MATTERS TO HISTORY.

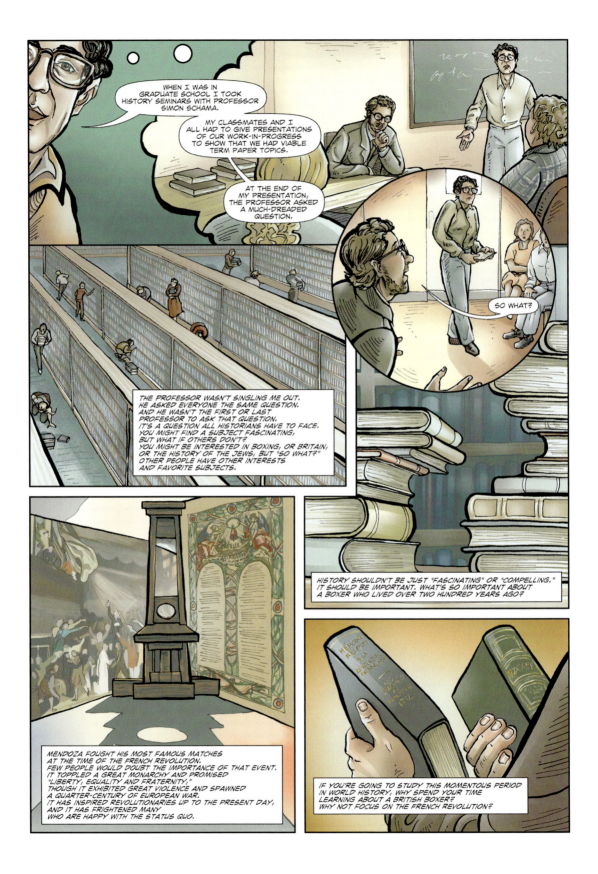

WHEN I WAS IN GRADUATE SCHOOL I TOOK HISTORY SEMINARS WITH PROFESSOR SIMON SCHAMA.

MY CLASSMATES AND I ALL HAD TO GIVE PRESENTATIONS OF OUR WORK-IN-PROGRESS TO SHOW THAT WE HAD VIABLE TERM PAPER TOPICS.

AT THE END OF MY PRESENTATION, THE PROFESSOR ASKED A MUCH-DREADED QUESTION.

SO WHAT?

THE PROFESSOR WASN'T SINGLING ME OUT. HE ASKED EVERYONE THE SAME QUESTION. AND HE WASN'T THE FIRST OR LAST PROFESSOR TO ASK THAT QUESTION. IT'S A QUESTION ALL HISTORIANS HAVE TO FACE. YOU MIGHT FIND A SUBJECT FASCINATING, BUT WHAT IF OTHERS DON'T? YOU MIGHT BE INTERESTED IN BOXING, OR BRITAIN, OR THE HISTORY OF THE JEWS, BUT "SO WHAT?" OTHER PEOPLE HAVE OTHER INTERESTS AND FAVORITE SUBJECTS.

HISTORY SHOULDN'T BE JUST "FASCINATING" OR "COMPELLING." IT SHOULD BE IMPORTANT. WHAT'S SO IMPORTANT ABOUT A BOXER WHO LIVED OVER TWO HUNDRED YEARS AGO?

MENDOZA FOUGHT HIS MOST FAMOUS MATCHES AT THE TIME OF THE FRENCH REVOLUTION. FEW PEOPLE WOULD DOUBT THE IMPORTANCE OF THAT EVENT. IT TOPPLED A GREAT MONARCHY AND PROMISED "LIBERTY, EQUALITY AND FRATERNITY," THOUGH IT EXHIBITED GREAT VIOLENCE AND SPAWNED A QUARTER-CENTURY OF EUROPEAN WAR. IT HAS INSPIRED REVOLUTIONARIES UP TO THE PRESENT DAY, AND IT HAS FRIGHTENED MANY WHO ARE HAPPY WITH THE STATUS QUO.

IF YOU'RE GOING TO STUDY THIS MOMENTOUS PERIOD IN WORLD HISTORY, WHY SPEND YOUR TIME LEARNING ABOUT A BRITISH BOXER? WHY NOT FOCUS ON THE FRENCH REVOLUTION?

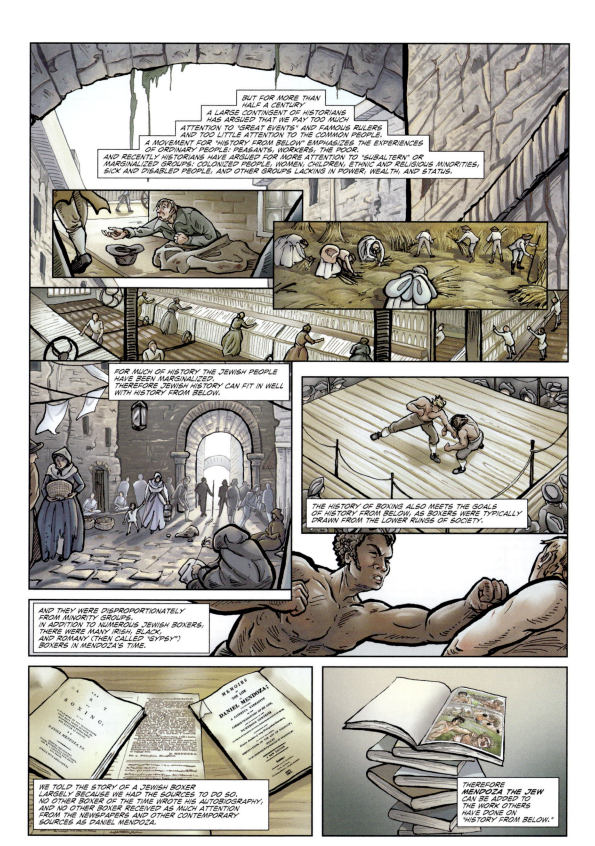

BUT FOR MORE THAN HALF A CENTURY A LARGE CONTINGENT OF HISTORIANS HAS ARGUED THAT WE PAY TOO MUCH ATTENTION TO "GREAT EVENTS" AND FAMOUS RULERS AND TOO LITTLE ATTENTION TO THE COMMON PEOPLE. A MOVEMENT FOR "HISTORY FROM BELOW" EMPHASIZES THE EXPERIENCES OF ORDINARY PEOPLE: PEASANTS, WORKERS, THE POOR, AND RECENTLY HISTORIANS HAVE ARGUED FOR MORE ATTENTION TO "SUBALTERN" OR MARGINALIZED GROUPS: COLONIZED PEOPLE, WOMEN, CHILDREN, ETHNIC AND RELIGIOUS MINORITIES, SICK AND DISABLED PEOPLE, AND OTHER GROUPS LACKING IN POWER, WEALTH, AND STATUS.

FOR MUCH OF HISTORY THE JEWISH PEOPLE HAVE BEEN MARGINALIZED. THEREFORE JEWISH HISTORY CAN FIT IN WELL WITH HISTORY FROM BELOW.

THE HISTORY OF BOXING ALSO MEETS THE GOALS OF HISTORY FROM BELOW, AS BOXERS WERE TYPICALLY DRAWN FROM THE LOWER RUNGS OF SOCIETY.

AND THEY WERE DISPROPORTIONATELY FROM MINORITY GROUPS. IN ADDITION TO NUMEROUS JEWISH BOXERS, THERE WERE MANY IRISH, BLACK, AND ROMANY (THEN CALLED "GYPSY") BOXERS IN MENDOZA'S TIME.

WE TOLD THE STORY OF A JEWISH BOXER LARGELY BECAUSE WE HAD THE SOURCES TO DO SO. NO OTHER BOXER OF THE TIME WROTE HIS AUTOBIOGRAPHY, AND NO OTHER BOXER RECEIVED AS MUCH ATTENTION FROM THE NEWSPAPERS AND OTHER CONTEMPORARY SOURCES AS DANIEL MENDOZA.

THEREFORE MENDOZA THE JEW CAN BE ADDED TO THE WORK OTHERS HAVE DONE ON "HISTORY FROM BELOW."

WE HAVE TOLD YOU A STORY ABOUT BOXERS AND JEWS, BUT WE HAVE ALSO TOLD YOU A STORY ABOUT BRITAIN.

YOU HAVE LEARNED ABOUT RELATIONS BETWEEN THE CLASSES, POPULAR LEISURE ACTIVITIES, AND THE ROLE OF SPORTS IN BRITISH SOCIETY.

AND YOU HAVE LEARNED ABOUT WHAT MANY BRITISH PEOPLE WERE THINKING AND TALKING ABOUT.

WHEN HISTORIANS EXAMINE SOURCES FROM THE PAST, THEY HAVE TO BE CAREFUL NOT TO ASSUME THEY KNOW WHAT PEOPLE WERE THINKING ON THE BASIS OF WHAT THEY *SHOULD* HAVE BEEN THINKING.

IT'S EASY TO ASSUME THAT BRITISH PEOPLE IN THE LATE 1700s MUST HAVE BEEN THINKING ABOUT FRANCE, SINCE WE KNOW IN RETROSPECT HOW IMPORTANT THE FRENCH REVOLUTION WAS.

1789	May Meeting of the Estates General
	June Deputies of the Third Estate (Commoners) declare themselves a National Assembly
	July Storming of the Bastille Prison
1791	September A revolutionary Constitution is completed
1793	January King Louis XVI is executed for treason
	September Reign of Terror begins
1794	July Robespierre executed, Reign of Terror ends

AND THEY WERE THINKING ABOUT FRANCE. BUT THEY WERE THINKING ABOUT OTHER THINGS AS WELL. AND SOURCES SUCH AS NEWSPAPERS CAN TELL US WHAT THOSE OTHER THINGS WERE.

HUMPHREYS and MENDOZA.

(Received by Express from STILTON *this Morning.)*

The long expected battle between Humphreys and Mendoza yesterday took place at Stilton. A spacious amphitheatre was erected for the purpose of seeing this contest in the Park of Mr. Thornton. It consisted of an erection of seats round a space of forty-eight feet in circumference, raised one above another, and capable of holding between two and three thousand persons. About that number of spectators were present, the highest seat was reserved for those who chose to see the combat ...

Humphreys appeared ... with Johnson as ... ame we did not ... Mr. Coombs as his Umpire. Mendoza soon afterwards entered the field of action, attended by his second, Capt. Brown, his bottle-holder Ryan, and his Umpire Sir Thomas Apppryce. They stripped, and on setting to, the seconds retired to the separate corners of the inclosure, according to the previous agreement of both parties.

Humphreys first struck at his antagonist in the face. The blow was stopped, and Mendoza *returned* with great quickness, and knocked him down. The second and third rounds were terminated in exactly the same manner. And after a contest for about forty minutes, in which Mendoza had evidently the advantage—generally catching his adversary's blows on his arm, and knocking him down or throwing him —a cessation was put to the battle by a circumstance which created much confusion among all parties.

In the *twenty-second* round Mendoza struck at Humphreys, on which the latter dropped. As the articles of agreement specified, that he who fell without a blow should lose the battle, a general cry of "Foul! Foul!" took place, and Mendoza's friends declared that he had won it.

Humphreys himself, if actuated by his well known liberality, will allow that his adversary fought with wonderful science and intrepidity.

FRANCE.

STATES GENERAL.

According to the last official advices, the Assembly was positively to meet on Tuesday the 5th inst. for the dispatch of business.

A meeting of the three estates was held on the 23d ult. but merely to chuse their officers. It was attended by 300 of the Clergy, 107 Nobles, and 336 Members of the third Estate. Some confusion arose in respect to the manner of certifying the Commissions of the Members, which took up nearly the whole day. They were then proceeding to the administration of the oath and other ceremonies, when a motion was made by the principal magistrate of Paris, to adjourn the meeting to the 28th.

This was very strongly objected to, and some Members said there would be danger in doing so. The government party however carried it, though many Members would not go away till midnight.

The Nobility have chosen the Duke de Tonnere their President, and M. d'Espremenil and M. Tolendal, as Secretaries. The Parisians denominate these *Fire* and *Water*. The third Estate has elected M. Target, President, and M. Baillot and Guillotin, Secretaries.

The Dresses to be worn by the Members of this Assembly are : the Bishops *rochet et camail*, a long white linen robe thrown over their shoulders fringed, with a Capuchin velvet cap :— the other Clergy nearly the same, with square caps. The Nobility loak of the sa ... stockings, crav ... feathers. If in ... silk and muslin cravat, and if in very deep mourning, the dress to be black cloth, crape cravat, and the hat cock'd *a la Henri quatre.*

"GREAT EVENTS" ARE NOT ALL THERE IS TO HISTORY. WHAT PEOPLE WERE THINKING IN THE PAST IS ALSO HISTORY.

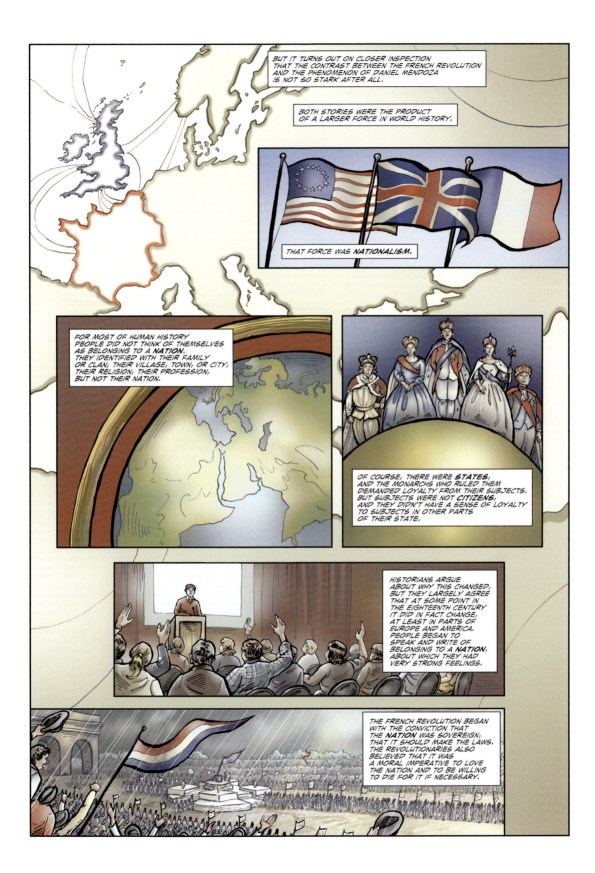

BUT IT TURNS OUT ON CLOSER INSPECTION THAT THE CONTRAST BETWEEN THE FRENCH REVOLUTION AND THE PHENOMENON OF DANIEL MENDOZA IS NOT SO STARK AFTER ALL.

BOTH STORIES WERE THE PRODUCT OF A LARGER FORCE IN WORLD HISTORY.

THAT FORCE WAS **NATIONALISM**.

FOR MOST OF HUMAN HISTORY PEOPLE DID NOT THINK OF THEMSELVES AS BELONGING TO A **NATION**. THEY IDENTIFIED WITH THEIR FAMILY OR CLAN, THEIR VILLAGE, TOWN, OR CITY; THEIR RELIGION; THEIR PROFESSION; BUT NOT THEIR NATION.

OF COURSE, THERE WERE **STATES**, AND THE MONARCHS WHO RULED THEM DEMANDED LOYALTY FROM THEIR SUBJECTS. BUT SUBJECTS WERE NOT **CITIZENS**, AND THEY DIDN'T HAVE A SENSE OF LOYALTY TO SUBJECTS IN OTHER PARTS OF THEIR STATE.

HISTORIANS ARGUE ABOUT WHY THIS CHANGED, BUT THEY LARGELY AGREE THAT AT SOME POINT IN THE EIGHTEENTH CENTURY IT DID IN FACT CHANGE, AT LEAST IN PARTS OF EUROPE AND AMERICA. PEOPLE BEGAN TO SPEAK AND WRITE OF BELONGING TO A **NATION**; ABOUT WHICH THEY HAD VERY STRONG FEELINGS.

THE FRENCH REVOLUTION BEGAN WITH THE CONVICTION THAT THE **NATION** WAS SOVEREIGN; THAT IT SHOULD MAKE THE LAWS. THE REVOLUTIONARIES ALSO BELIEVED THAT IT WAS A MORAL IMPERATIVE TO LOVE THE NATION AND TO BE WILLING TO DIE FOR IT IF NECESSARY.

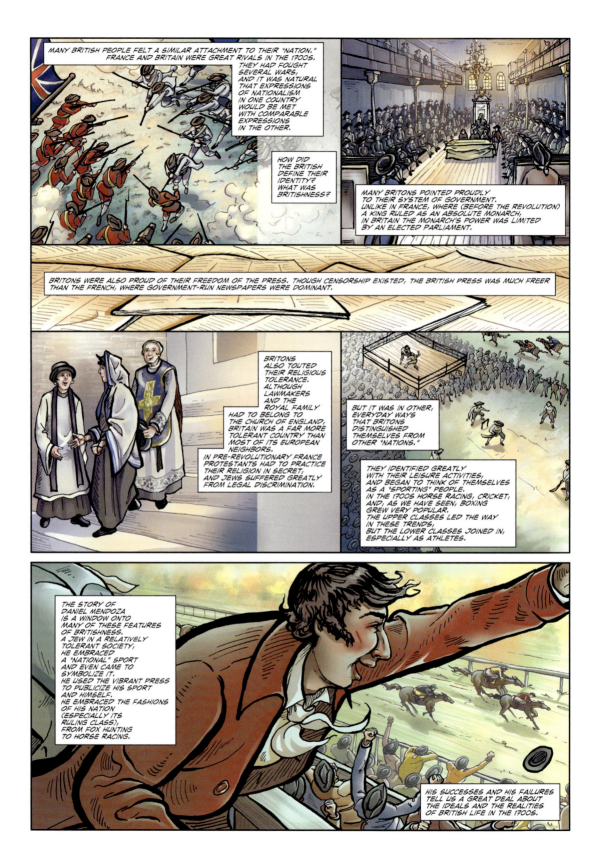

MANY BRITISH PEOPLE FELT A SIMILAR ATTACHMENT TO THEIR "NATION." FRANCE AND BRITAIN WERE GREAT RIVALS IN THE 1700S. THEY HAD FOUGHT SEVERAL WARS, AND IT WAS NATURAL THAT EXPRESSIONS OF NATIONALISM IN ONE COUNTRY WOULD BE MET WITH COMPARABLE EXPRESSIONS IN THE OTHER.

HOW DID THE BRITISH DEFINE THEIR IDENTITY? WHAT WAS BRITISHNESS?

MANY BRITONS POINTED PROUDLY TO THEIR SYSTEM OF GOVERNMENT. UNLIKE IN FRANCE, WHERE (BEFORE THE REVOLUTION) A KING RULED AS AN ABSOLUTE MONARCH, IN BRITAIN THE MONARCH'S POWER WAS LIMITED BY AN ELECTED PARLIAMENT.

BRITONS WERE ALSO PROUD OF THEIR FREEDOM OF THE PRESS. THOUGH CENSORSHIP EXISTED, THE BRITISH PRESS WAS MUCH FREER THAN THE FRENCH, WHERE GOVERNMENT-RUN NEWSPAPERS WERE DOMINANT.

BRITONS ALSO TOUTED THEIR RELIGIOUS TOLERANCE. ALTHOUGH LAWMAKERS AND THE ROYAL FAMILY HAD TO BELONG TO THE CHURCH OF ENGLAND, BRITAIN WAS A FAR MORE TOLERANT COUNTRY THAN MOST OF ITS EUROPEAN NEIGHBORS. IN PRE-REVOLUTIONARY FRANCE PROTESTANTS HAD TO PRACTICE THEIR RELIGION IN SECRET, AND JEWS SUFFERED GREATLY FROM LEGAL DISCRIMINATION.

BUT IT WAS IN OTHER, EVERYDAY WAYS THAT BRITONS DISTINGUISHED THEMSELVES FROM OTHER "NATIONS."

THEY IDENTIFIED GREATLY WITH THEIR LEISURE ACTIVITIES, AND BEGAN TO THINK OF THEMSELVES AS A "SPORTING" PEOPLE. IN THE 1700S HORSE RACING, CRICKET, AND, AS WE HAVE SEEN, BOXING GREW VERY POPULAR. THE UPPER CLASSES LED THE WAY IN THESE TRENDS, BUT THE LOWER CLASSES JOINED IN, ESPECIALLY AS ATHLETES.

THE STORY OF DANIEL MENDOZA IS A WINDOW ONTO MANY OF THESE FEATURES OF BRITISHNESS. A JEW IN A RELATIVELY TOLERANT SOCIETY, HE EMBRACED A "NATIONAL" SPORT AND EVEN CAME TO SYMBOLIZE IT. HE USED THE VIBRANT PRESS TO PUBLICIZE HIS SPORT AND HIMSELF. HE EMBRACED THE FASHIONS OF HIS NATION (ESPECIALLY ITS RULING CLASS), FROM FOX HUNTING TO HORSE RACING.

HIS SUCCESSES AND HIS FAILURES TELL US A GREAT DEAL ABOUT THE IDEALS AND THE REALITIES OF BRITISH LIFE IN THE 1700S.

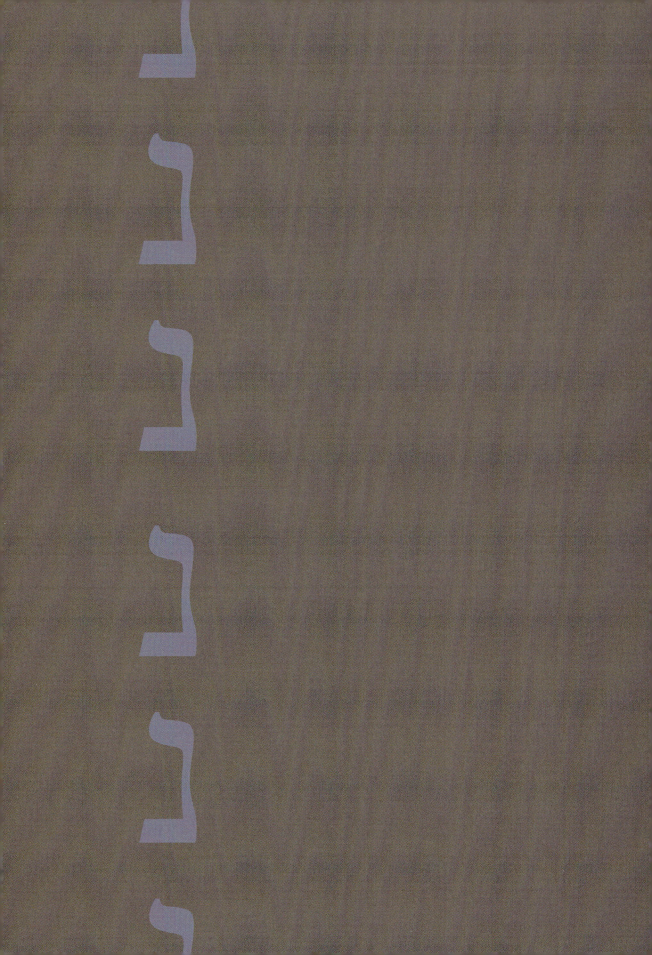

PART II
THE PRIMARY SOURCES

The graphic history you have just read is what historians call a *secondary source*. It is secondary because it was produced after the event and based on *primary sources*, or sources that date from the time of the historical subject in question. In order to produce the secondary source, the author has read hundreds of newspaper articles and other contemporary, in other words, primary, sources about Mendoza and his world, and the artist has looked at hundreds of images (everything from boxing rings to pubs to clothing to architecture) of British social life in the 1700s. The following is a sampling of primary sources. They are arranged in three groups, one for each of the three prizefights between Mendoza and Humphries. Examine them carefully. They will give you a better understanding of the story you have just read. They will fill in some gaps and give you a finer feel for how contemporaries understood the events and phenomena covered in the graphic history. And in Part V of this book you will have an opportunity to use the primary sources to construct your own interpretation. History does not come ready-made. You have to build it yourself. Primary sources are the building blocks.

SECTION 1. SOURCES ON THE ODIHAM MATCH

DOCUMENT 1.1. THE AGREEMENT

Mendoza is ready to fight Mr. Humphries on the 9th of January, 1788, for fifty pounds, twenty-five pounds to be staked, upon a stage of twenty-four feet square, to fight without dropping, unless by a blow, under penalty of forfeiting the whole fifty pounds.

No quarrel between the seconds to be a hindrance to the fight; the party that may begin the quarrel to forfeit the money.

The door-money to be equally shared.

No person to be admitted on the stage but seconds, bottle-holders, and umpires.

The place to be mutually agreed upon.

The remaining twenty-five pounds to be made good this day fortnight in the hands of the present stake-holder, who has received fifty pounds, or the deposit to be forfeited.

Source: *Whitehall Evening Post* (London), December 6–8, 1787.

DOCUMENT 1.2. A REPORT IN THE *LONDON CHRONICLE*

Farther Particulars relative to the Fight between HUMHPRIES *and* Mendoza.

There existed, previous to this contest, a rooted antipathy between the parties, which, during the time it continued, a person superficially skilled in physiognomy might easily have discovered; in the countenance of Mendoza there was a kind of contemptuous laugh; on that of Humphries there appeared an implacable hatred of his adversary. Humphries treated the Jew with the greatest indifference before the contest, and declared that he could not possibly suffer it to continue above five minutes. The result of the battle proved this positive assertion erroneous, for he was for the space of 20 minutes perpetually retreating from the impetuosity of the Jew's movements, who forced him to every corner of the stage, and gave him a decisive blow, that occasioned the fence of the stage to give way, and by which the back of Humphreys was excoriated. In the course of the encounter, Johnson stepped in between the combatants, and prevented Mendoza following up a blow which probably might have produced a material turn in the contest. Perhaps the most refined effort of skill, on the part of Mendoza, was presented at the period when Humphries jumped up to frustrate the guard; but Mendoza, apprised of his design, stopped, and, in the twinkling of an eye, put in several potent blows on the body of his adversary.

The Jew, in the early part of the contest, exhibited a great share of the *vis comica* in his aspect; for whenever his opponent missed his aim, he laughed at him with a conscious superiority of his power of defence. Respecting the betts, less was lost than was expected, for the knowing tribe edged in the early part of the battle: all the odds that they had laid were diminished by the temporary success of Mendoza.

In the abatement of the exquisite skill displayed in the conflict, we must observe, that Mendoza acted unworthy of himself, for when closed in with Humphries, he screwed his nose, and thrust his knuckles in his eye. This he did, report says, by way of retaliation; for his antagonist, conscious of his superior strength, frequently endeavoured to frustrate the skill of his adversary, by closing in upon him.

Mendoza had obvious disadvantage in the choice of his second, who was greatly inferior in point of stage-trick, to the veteran Johnson. Ryan, who recently fought the latter, offered to second Mendoza, which, however, he refused, being more desirous of trusting a Jew than a Christian, on the occasion.

Mendoza, from the blow given him under the ear, swallowed more blood than he evacuated.

The *amateurs* present, were Colonel Fitzpatrick, Captain Aston, Alderman Newnham, Mr. Shum, and Mr. Hervey Coombe. Mr. Hopner, who executed the portrait of Humphries, was also on the spot. Mr. Bradyll was in the town, but not a spectator of the action.

The victory of Humphries is rather to be imputed to the accident of Mendoza's straining his ancle, the anguish of which made him faint, than to the effect of the last blow, however well placed. The Jew finding himself from the violent extension of the sinews of his leg, which swelled exceedingly, unable to stand, without support, wisely resigned the palm to his adversary.

Had Mendoza beat Humphries, it was his intention, immediately on his return to town to have gone before the Lord Mayor, and have made an affidavit, that he would never again fight a pitched battle; but having, from accident proved unsuccessful, it is generally expected he will again challenge his victorious opponent.

Humphries came from Odiham yesterday, and Mendoza, and his second, David Benjamin (the Jew pastry cook), are hourly expected in Duke's place.

The origin of the dispute between the Jew and Christian boxers, rose from the following circumstance. Some time past, Mendoza, being in want of cash, borrowed 20 [pounds] of a gentleman *amateur* of the science, under the idea of its being a deposit for an intended battle. This coming to the knowledge of Humphries he waited on the lender, and informed him, that he had been imposed on, no battle being intended; in consequence of this discovery, Mendoza was arrested at the suit of the gentleman, by Humphries, who is a bailiff's follower. This transaction Mendoza never forgave.

Mr. Bradyl [*sic*], the patron of Humphries, and who highly esteems him for the decency of his manners, was not present at the battle, but sent his servant to bring him the earliest accounts of the event of the conflict. The messenger arrived in town about nine o'clock with a letter from Humphries, which was delivered to Mr. Bradyl at Cramer's concert. It was nearly as follows:

"Sir,

"I have *done* the *Jew,* and am in good *health* at this present writing. HUMPHRIES."

Humphries did not strike one stroke for four that he received, and yet such was the superior efficacy of his blows, and the consequence of scientific direction, that at the end of the battle the Jew was completely exhausted, and so sickened by the blows he had received, as to be carried off the stage lifeless, while Humphries was nothing impaired.

Source: *London Chronicle* (London), January 10–12, 1788.

DOCUMENT 1.3. A REPORT IN THE *MORNING HERALD*

HUMPHRIES AND MENDOZA.

Of the little topics which occasionally agitate the public mind, few have excited more attention than the present combat. The known science of each antagonist—their muscular prowess, and their repeated victories, joined to the prevailing passion for this exercise, occasioned in the bosoms of numbers the most eager anxiety.

But what is yet more whimsical—*Christianity* and *Juadism* [sic] were actually set in opposition to each other, and those who never thought of *religion* in any other shape, were interested for those who were supposed to champion the cause of their respective *creeds*.

But there were yet more substantial reasons for this anxiety, as *twenty-five thousand pounds* were actually staked on the issue of the combat, by the inhabitants of *Duke's Place* only.—Then "Tell it not in *Gath*—repeat it not in the streets of *Askelon*"—the victory has fallen to the share of the *Christian!*

In the presence of a thousand persons assembled yesterday morning, in an enclosed spacious piece of ground at Odiham, in Hampshire, the grand contest between *Mendoza* and *Humphries* was decided.

About five minutes after one o'clock the combatants mounted the stage; Mendoza, with Isaacs his second, and the bottle holder; and *Humphries*, with Johnson for his second and Tring bottle-holder.

The stage, previous to the commencement of the Fight was exceedingly wet, which rendered it necessary to scatter saw-dust, rosin, and chalk over it, in order that the parties might stand firmly. Mr. Allen, the Brewer, was appointed umpire by Humphries; and a Jew merchant was nominated to the same office by Mendoza.

The first blow was struck by the latter, near the eye of his opponent, which he followed up most successfully for some minutes; and at the onset of the encounter Mendoza appeared, in every respect, to possess a superiority of science and strength over Humphries.—This opinion he preserved, with the surrounding spectators, for upwards of twenty minutes;—in the course of which time he displayed as wonderful dexterity in stopping the blows of his adversary, as he did strength and firmness in the effect of them.

The odds were at that time, one hundred pounds to sixty in favour of the Jew, which very soon afterwards altered as much to the advantage of Humphries, in consequence of his having successfully directed several powerful blows at his adversary.

At this juncture of the conflict, Humphries appeared to gain ground, and the odds ran very much in his favor, but still more after he had put in a blow under the left ear of Mendoza, which occasioned an effusion of blood to gush from his mouth.

After this, however, the Jew struck several blows about the eyes of his antagonist, which had nearly blinded him.—Humphries' vigour, at this period, seemed entirely unabated, and shortly after he gave Mendoza a stroke on the pit of the stomach, which he had, during the whole of the contest, aimed to accomplish.

This blow brought Mendoza down, with great violence, on the stage—and terminated the victory in favor of Humphries.—The Jew appeared to labor under very great torture from the blows he had received—fainted away on the stage—and was afterwards borne off by his friends from the scene of action.

Mendoza fought nobly, and gave the spectators such an admirable specimen of the modern art of boxing, as drew down the repeated huzzas of the multitude, and although in the combat he was fairly conquered, yet the reputation he has gained by it, is such as will prove highly profitable to his professional pursuits; Humphries, though meriting the highest praise for his knowledge of the art, is unquestionably inferior to the Jew in point of science, but superior in strength. The contest lasted twenty-nine minutes.

Source: *Morning Herald* (London), Thursday, January 10, 1788.

DOCUMENT 1.4. A REPORT IN THE *MORNING POST AND DAILY ADVERTISER*

BOXING.

HUMPHRIES and MENDOZA.

SECONDS,

JOHNSON AND D. BENJAMIN.

BOTTLE-HOLDERS,

TRING and HELSEA.

UMPIRES,

ALLEN & MORAVIA.

The long-expected BATTLE between HUMPHRIES and Mendoza was decided yesterday at ODIHAM, in *Hampshire,* without any interruption on the part of the Justices.

A stage was erected by *One o'clock. Humphries* mounted it immediately; and *Mendoza* appeared in a few moments after.

There was a door to the stage; and the admission was *half a guinea* each. About *four hundred* persons paid; and nearly *eight hundred* were present.

The money collected for admission was equally divided between the combatants.

Previous to the battle, the odds were *three* to *one* in favour of *Humphries*.

At *twenty minutes* past *one* o'clock, the *sett-to* began, which was judged to have been the *neatest* that ever had been seen on a stage—even in the days of BROUGHTON.—It lasted some minutes before any offer, excepting *feints*, was made.

Mendoza struck the first blow, in doing which, he fell on his back, in consequence of the stage being very wet with the rain.

The second blow that *Mendoza* struck, brought *Humphries* down, and drew blood from his nose.

In the next *round* they closed, and *Mendoza* threw *Humphries*.

Mendoza gained much at this time, and *kept the lead* for nearly a quarter of an hour.

This advantage is not altogether to be attributed to superiority in the *Jew*, but in some measure to the *wetness* of the *stage*, which prevented *Humphries* from *keeping his legs*, not withstanding *saw-dust* was continually thrown on it.

The odds at this time changed greatly in favour of *Mendoza*, and *two* and *three* to *one* were betted.

The slippers which Humphries wore were then taken off, and he obtained a pair of *worsted stockings*, which being put on, he found he could *keep his legs*.

Humphries received many falls; but recovering himself, he soon *came about*, and had greatly the advantage in the four following *rounds*.

The bets at this time were even.

In one of these rounds, *Humphries* threw *Mendoza* a *cross-buttock*, and pitched him on his face, which cut his forehead just above the right eye, and bruised his nose.

He, however, recovered a little, so as to give *Humphries* a blow in the face; but slipping at the same time, and falling with *his leg under him, sprained his ancle,—when* he immediately GAVE IN.

The battle was fought on both sides with wonderful skill and ability.

Mendoza appeared to be in greater practice than *Humphries,* which is not extraordinary, as he has fought *five* battles within *fourteen* months.

He *put in* more blows than *Humphries,* and *stopped* in a very capital style.

Humphries, after the second *round,* for some time fought only on the defensive, and struck but seldom, though his blows were made with much greater force than those of his antagonist.

The *Jew* undoubtedly evinced the greatest skill, and for some time was the strongest, but the *game* of *Humphries*—which is scarcely to be equalled—supported him in a very extraordinary manner, and, on recovering his *wind,* he appeared much stronger than his adversary.

It was said that *Humphries* could have fought *Mendoza* half an hour longer, had the latter not *given in.*

There was a dispute, in consequence of a *foul blow* by *Mendoza,* but *Humphries nobly* ended the controversy by allowing it to be fair.

One of *Humphries'* eyes was hurt, by *Mendoza's screwing his thumb* into it, which he in closing did, and also, *pulled and scratched* Humphries *nose.*

The contest lasted *twenty eight minutes and fifty four seconds,* during which time the *Jew* knocked down *Humphries oftenest.*

Immediately after *Mendoza* had *given in,* he fainted, and was carried off the stage.

Although *Humphries* was not cut in the face so much as *Mendoza,* yet his eyes were closed.

The first *round* lasted *two* minutes; and two or three other rounds in the course of the battle continued *four* minutes.

Mendoza's blows were *straight;*—those of *Humphries* were *round.*

Credit is due to the *Jew* for his *skill,* and to the *Christian* for his *courage.*

On *Mendoza* declining to fight any more, *Humphries* challenged his second, which was refused.

It is expected that another battle will take place between these two boxers, and that *Mendoza* will be the challenger.

Source: *Morning Post and Daily Advertiser* (London), Thursday, January 10, 1788.

DOCUMENT 1.5. A REPORT IN THE *WHITEHALL EVENING POST*

BOXING and ABOUT IT.

HUMPHRIES and MENDOZA.

Where the Art depends so much on its *celerity,* it is as difficult to *catch* observation as blows. What has been caught on the late celebrated contest, between Christianity and Judaism, is as follows:

As a *Professor,* Mendoza, though beaten, has acquired more fame than he has lost. He certainly hit Humphries oftener than Humphries hit him: in *close fighting*—much oftener still. In strength of arm he seems to have the advantage; and, when struggling, he kept down the head of his antagonist and at that time hurt him most. He here endeavoured to force his knuckles into the *eye* of Humphries; and, what is singular, more than once—*pulled him by the nose till it bled.*

In his standing up—in the *first position*—speaking according to Art—Mendoza kept his guard closer to his body, and by that measure gave a *greater momentum* to the arm when struck out. He stopped blows to the full as well as Humphries.

In manliness of manner—in grace of position—in judgment, and in force of blow, he was much inferior to Humphries indeed. In point of personal courage too, and contempt of himself, Humphries likewise had the advantage.

In point of throwing falls—the advantage, which was supposed to lie on the side of Humphries, was entirely transferred to Mendoza; whose activity agreed better with the slippery state in which the rain had left the stage.

Humphries fell down six times successively, owing to this circumstance; and gave to Mendoza an appearance of superiority, which was more seeming than real.

In point of Boxing—the superiority was difficult to ascertain—though the character and style of each was very ascertainable.

In the defensive position—Humphries held his arms more out at length; and though he kept his antagonist at a distance by that method, yet he lost the advantage of striking quick.

In point of manly and fine attitude—every posture of Humphries—was grace itself: and if ever the character of the English Boxer, like that of the Roman Gladiator, is to be transmitted to posterity—the eye, the countenance, the posture, and the nerve of Humphries, should be selected for that picture, to succeeding times.

From the numbers, both of fashion and of fortune, as well as of the common people—the present taste of the country may be estimated—and manly exercise is the character of it.

Humphries did not strike one stroke for four that he received, and yet such was the superior efficacy of his blows, and the consequence of scientific direction, that at the end of the battle the Jew was completely exhausted, and so sickened by the blows he had received, as to be carried off the stage lifeless, while Humphries was nothing impaired.

In the late assemblage at Odiham, no magistrate interfered; and yet no disturbance followed, no riot ensued: which proved what we have often asserted, that no scene is more quiet—than a public Boxing-Match. On the contrary side, the emoluments to the town were very large indeed.

In the town of Bagshot, more than three hundred persons slept in their way to the battle, on Tuesday night. At the little town of Hooke, seven Fashionable Gentlemen slept—in the hay loft.

Above twenty carriages returned to town, from the impossibility of getting horses—though any money was offered for them.

Source: *Whitehall Evening Post* (London), January 10–12, 1788.

DOCUMENT 1.6. A REPORT IN THE *WORLD*

THE BOXING MATCH.

ODIHAM, HAMPSHIRE.

HUMPHRIES AND MENDOZA.

By the attention of a Gentleman of that town, a place very singular for its convenience in seeing, was prepared for the exhibition of this long ex-pected Battle. It was a Paddock surrounded by a high wall, which on two sides of it had a raised terrace, capable of holding perhaps five or six hun-dred people.

There were about that number there—though the price of admittance was *half-a-guinea.*

A Stage of twenty-four feet square was completely finished by half past twelve. At one o'clock—HUMPHRIES came upon the Stage, attended by *Johnson* as his Second, and *Tring* as his Bottle-holder.

The sight of him raised the odds from *two to one,* at which they had stood some time, to *five to two*—as doubts had been spread, of his condi-tion and state of health.

In a few minutes after, MENDOZA made his appearance, with *David Benjamin* as his Second, and another Jew as his Bottle-holder.

At five minutes past *one o'clock,* they were put up to each other. But so cautious were both of giving advantage, that many minutes elapsed be-fore either received a blow—and a shower of rain having fallen just before they began, the Stage was so slippery, that both fell before either of them received any blow of consequence. Which gave the first *knocking down blow,* was disputed; but the superior quickness of striking, was soon seen to be in MENDOZA; for whenever they closed, the Jew always hit *Humphries*—and generally fell uppermost, from his activity.

After fighting thirteen minutes—the odds ran *three to two* in favour of *Mendoza;* and were offered very vociferously.

The change encouraged MENDOZA, but did not discourage his Antagonist—who preserved his coolness and intrepidity as perfectly as at first;—and after a contest of *twenty-four minutes and an half,* Mendoza *gave in*—and HUMPHRIES was *declared the Conqueror.*

The *Jew's* style of fighting was very different from that of his adver-sary. He fought low, and with cunning: with much dexterity, but without grace—While the look and attitudes of *Humphries,* continually presented those beauties which a Painter would have arrested every moment, to make them his own.

The gallantry of his spirit too, was not less conspicuous; for twice, when there was an idea of Mendoza doing something unfair, and *the Umpires* were enquiring about it—HUMPHRIES gave it against himself—and said, his antagonist had hit him as he ought to do.

At the end of the Battle, HUMPHRIES was carried off in triumph on the shoulders of his friends—but he would not leave MENDOZA, without sitting down by him, and telling him how well he had fought.

MENDOZA seemed much weakened at the last, and he had sprained his ancle very violently.

Of the AMATEURS—the number was very great;—most of the fashionable men of London, with many others from Bath, and all the adjacent counties.

Of the *Casualties*—was that of Mr. PRICE having his pocket picked of twenty-five pounds.

Of the scenes on the road—with some *in Beds,* and some *without*—carriages, without a horse to be had—rooms with twenty people sleeping upon the carpets, and many gentlemen reduced to walk the last fourteen miles—all these furnished a second representation of the *Stratford Jubilee*—equally noisy, equally crowded, equally wished to be seen.

The collection at the door was supposed to amount to *one hundred and fifty,* or *two hundred pounds*, which was to be divided between the Combatants—who well merited it, as having given the most *Scientific display* of the Art *and* ADDRESS *of* BOXING, that ever was exhibited.

We trust this gradual encrease of the manly character, will in short time be honoured with a regular *Amphi-Theatre in the* METROPOLIS.

Source: *World* (London), Thursday, January 10, 1788.

DOCUMENT 1.7. MENDOZA'S FIRST LETTER TO THE EDITOR (INCLUDING DR. SAFFORY'S LETTER)

Mr. MENDOZA'S *Letter in Vindication of his Behaviour at the late* Contest *between him and* Mr. HUPHREYS.

Understanding, with no little degree of anxiety, that some gentlemen have disputed the propriety of my conduct, on Wednesday last, in the battle between Mr. Humphreys and myself, I am induced to exhibit the following facts; on the proof of which, I will hazard every credit from a generous Public, whom I never have, and never will deceive.

At ten minutes after one o'clock, I set to with Mr. Humphreys, and, for nearly 20 minutes, I had most evidently the superiority. Finding with ease I could stop most of his blows, and though I was frequently closed by Mr. Humphreys, (a mode of fighting I could wish to avoid) I found an ability to throw him.

My strength and spirits were superior to my adversary, till the last fall but two, when I fell directly on *my head,* and by the force, pitched quite over. I then found myself much hurt in my loins, indeed so much, that it was with extreme difficulty I could *stand up right;* but by the last fall I received, I was scarcely able to breathe; and it was with great pain that I could sit on the knee of my Second. When Johnson asked me, if I had done, I could only answer him by a sign.

By this untoward accident alone, I lost a battle, on which my warmest hopes were fixed.

To my friends and patrons on that occasion I owe much; to the public, I owe still more; the confidence of which I never have betrayed. With this assurance I shall only add, that if the world is desirous of renewing the conflict, and should Mr. Humphreys be willing, I shall be more than happy to engage him.

D. MENDOZA.

No. 9 *White-street, Houndsditch.*

P.S. Mr. Henry Saffory, surgeon, Devonshire-street, Bishopsgate-street, is the gentleman who now attends me. The following attestation Mr. Saffory has permitted me to publish:

At the immediate request of some gentlemen of my acquaintance, I visited Mr. Daniel Mendoza this morning on his return from Odiham. Having very minutely inspected his various bruises, and fully investigated his complaints; I do declare, from every appearance, that it was impossible for him any longer to maintain a conflict, in which he was so severely hurt. The seat of his complaint is in his loins; and I have no doubt but the excruciating pains he must then have experienced, was sufficient to deprive him of the ability to stand.

HENRY SAFFORY.

Thursday, Jan. 10, 1788.
Devonshire Street.

Source: *Whitehall Evening Post* (London), January 12–15, 1788.

DOCUMENT 1.8. HUMPHRIES'S LETTER TO THE EDITOR IN RESPONSE TO MENDOZA'S FIRST LETTER

Notwithstanding my declaration, previous to the Battle between me and Mr. *Mendoza*—that whether I was beaten, or I beat him, I would *never fight again;* yet, as in his Address to the Public, he has insinuated—that in his late contest with me, at ODIHAM, his being "*beaten was the mere effect of* ACCIDENT"—I do now declare, that I am ready to meet him at any time, not exceeding *three months* from the present date—on condition, that as it is merely to *oblige* him that I once more enter the lists with him, the sum we fight for, shall not be less than *two hundred and fifty guineas a side.*

The terms of fighting to be exactly the same as the last, excepting, that the *whole door money* shall go to the winner of the battle. The stakes to be held by the same gentleman as before.

RICHARD HUMPHREYS.

A copy of the above is sent to Mr. Mendoza, with a request, that he will give a positive answer before the expiration of the week; as his longer silence will be construed as a disinclination to renew the contest.

Jan. 14, 1788.

Source: *Whitehall Evening Post* (London), January 12–15, 1788.

DOCUMENT 1.9. MENDOZA'S LETTER TO THE EDITOR, JANUARY 16, 1788

Sir,

IT is with some concern, that I feel the least inducement to give a negative to the *challenge* of Mr. Humphreys; but I flatter myself I shall stand fully justified in the opinion of a candid public, when the conditions of that challenge are properly considered.

The first proposition of Mr. Humphreys, is *to fight for 250 guineas a-side.* This the public will readily perceive, is conveying (in an oblique direction) a negative in the challenge itself. The right of odds may very fairly be expected, both from the recent victory of Mr. Humphreys, and the opinion which the friends of that gentleman so warmly support, of his superior skill in the *art of boxing.* Yet I am bold to say, that neither these circumstances, nor any inconvenience the deposit of so large a sum may subject me to, shall prevent the contest.

The second proposition, is not altogether the most liberal; *to fight within three months.* Mr. Humphreys surely must be informed, that a complaint in the loins, is sometimes an unwelcome companion through life: the proposition on the one hand exhibits an [*sic*] hidden wish to prevent a contest, or on the other a want of feeling that can do little credit to his most sanguine friends.

The last proposition,—*the winner to have the door,* however it may breathe an affected sense of superiority on the side of Mr. Humphreys, I most cordially agree to. The time which was limited for my reply, *being one week,* is a circumstance, that will not impress the public with any additional opinion, either of the courage or candour of Mr. Humphreys.

As I have unavoidably denied my acceptance to the challenge of Mr. Humphreys, it may be expected, I should make some propositions myself:

which if they appear liberal in the public eye, I shall be indifferent to any answer he may convey; whether to meet me on the stage, or rather wear those laurels, with which *chance* has crowned him.

The first proposition is, that I will meet Mr. Humphreys on the same sized stage as at Odiham, *i.e.* 24 by 24, and fight him for *250 guineas a-side*.

The second proposition—the *victor shall have the door*. And as the world is decidedly of opinion that Mr. Humphreys is superior in the *art of boxing*, the third proposition that I make is, the *man who first closes shall be the loser*. The time of fighting, it is impossible to mention, since the injury I have received on my loins, may continue its effects to a distant period; by the moment I am relieved from that complaint, and declared capable by the gentleman who now attends me, I shall chearfully step forward, and appoint the day.

The acceptance or denial of Mr. Humphreys to the third proposition, will impress the public with an additional opinion of his superior skill, or they must conclude that he is somewhat conscious of his inferiority in scientific knowledge. In imitation of the challenge of Mr. Humphreys, I shall *not* distress him for an immediate reply: but leave him to consult his friends, and his own feelings, and send an answer at his leisure.

I remain, Sir,
Your obedient servant,
DANIEL Mendoza.

No. 9 White Street, Houndsditch, Jan. 16, 1788.

Source: *Whitehall Evening Post* (London), January 17–19, 1788.

DOCUMENT 1.10. HUMPHRIES'S LETTER TO THE EDITOR, JANUARY 20, 1788

Sir,

WITHOUT replying to the invidious reflections so bountifully bestowed on me by Mr. *Mendoza*, (which, unless we were to abide by *common sense*, must only expose us to the derision of a discerning public), I shall first observe,—that it affords me infinite pleasure, when I consider, after a week's reflection on my Answer to his Challenge, it does not contain a sentiment I could wish amended: And I mean unequivocally to abide by my first engagements, even to the *article of odds;* for how can he reconcile the justice of his remark on this head, with his assertion, *"that I am indebted to Chance for the Victory."*

Yet I cannot help remarking, that neither Mr. *Mendoza* nor his friends, seemed decided where they should fix this *unlucky disaster.* At first it was in *his ancle;* and there were people who would have sworn they saw three of the bones come out.—Then the disorder moved gradually to his hips; from whence, (lest it should be mistaken for a rheumatic complaint), it settled with most excruciating pains, in his loins; where I am aware it may abide as long as he finds it convenient.—His relying on his Surgeon for the moment when he shall be pronounced recovered, is ridiculous; his complaint being of such nature, that himself must be the best, and only judge, when he is free from it.

It *may* be true, what he observes of the strain in his loins, *"that it is sometimes an unwelcome companion through life;"*—but does it follow, that I am to stand engaged to meet him, whenever he shall think proper to call upon me? Is there no time when a man may be supposed past his prime for boxing? Or if not, shall he never have the choice of retiring from scenes, which at once involve the hazard of his life, and reputation?

The proposition which sentences, *"the first man who closes, to be the loser,"* I must confess does not more surprise me for its absurdity, than that it should come from the man, who in the last contest, was himself the *first to close*—not to mention the folly in depriving himself of the opportunity of *gougeing,* and practicing other unmanly arts, the effects of a defeated spirit. Whoever considers the above proposal, must be surprised it did not occur to him, to declare against *hard blows;* "a mode of fighting" he may also "wish to avoid"—But it is endless to trace his absurdities,—indeed, both his mode of reasoning, and the nature of his proposals, are such, that it is wonderful no one should have reminded him, that the offering them to the consideration of the Public, must be deemed an *insult,* where it cannot but be his interest, at least, to make a show of *respect.*

In fine, the sentiments of justice and liberality are readily conceived, and as easily conveyed:—Presuming on this, I thought that I gave sufficient time for a *direct* answer;—but to give colour to artifice, that it may bear the semblance of candour, requires *at least a week's meditation*—or, it would be too easily detected.

Once more, I repeat it, that I shall meet him only on the *conditions stated in my first letter;* with this ADDITIONAL ONE,

That should *I* be beaten through accident, he shall give me an opportunity of re-establishing my credit in another contest. It is clear, that should I accede to his ridiculous propositions, it would only be driving him to new straits—for the whole tenor of his Letter only proves, that *Parrying,* not *Fighting,* is the end of his wishes.

RICHARD HUMPRHEYS.

January 20, 1788.

Source: *World* (London), Tuesday, January 22, 1788.

DOCUMENT 1.11. MENDOZA'S LETTER TO THE EDITOR, JANUARY 23, 1788

Sir,

TO analyze the production of Mr. Humphreys, which appeared in your Paper of Tuesday last, would be a task, the result of which would furnish the public with but little information either useful or entertaining; yet, as there are a few points which deserve some comment, I shall stand excused in the opinion of the World for this intrusion.

The prefatory part of the address of Mr. Humphreys, is explicable only by the author; but his assertion—"that he is determined to abide unequivocally by his first engagements, for after a few week's [*sic*] reflection upon his challenge, it does not contain a sentiment he could wish to amend"—is a contradiction that *his* pretensions to *common sense*, surely should have taught him to avoid: if the addition of a new proposition to his former challenge, leaves it unequivocally the same, a catalogue of conditions, from the prolific invention of Mr. Humphreys, may soon follow (like the preceding) as the *intended* obstacles to any future battle.

The second paragraph in the letter of Mr. Humphreys, is a distant reflection on the surgeon who attends me; but his professional abilities are too eminent, to be affected by so pitiful an attempt. The only inducement I had to abide by the declaration of my surgeon, was to exempt me *from the charge* of being even able to make any artificial excuse. The same paragraph fully explains the propriety of that remark; for as a specimen of candid implication, Mr. Humphreys has inserted, *that the complaint in my loins may remain as long as I find it convenient.*

The subsequent paragraph must meet the general current of observation:—that however he may praise his good fortune for being led from the scene of battle with *his life,* he has, alas! too much reason to lament the loss of *reputation.*

However, to prevent Mr. Humphreys the apology of wasting his prime of life in the expectation of my recovery, *I will engage, at all hazards, to fight him by the Meeting in October.*

The assertion of Mr. Humphreys, that *I closed first,* is a positive falsehood; indeed, it is rather unfortunate, that this doctrine has remained so long silent: Its appearance in the Boxing-Calendar is so very ill-timed, that a candid world cannot pay it the least tribute of respect.

The opportunity of *gougeing,* and the practice of other unmanly arts, being totally done away in a scientific display of Boxing, should operate as assistant inducements to Mr. Humphreys to accept my challenge; particularly, since *hard blows must tell.* But the simple facts are there:—Mr. Humphreys is afraid; he dare not meet me as a Boxer:—he retires with the fullest conviction of his want of scientific knowledge; and though he has the *advantage of strength* and *age;*—though a *Teacher* of the *Art,* he meanly shrinks from a public trial of that skill, on which his bread depends.

To intrude any further on the indulgence of a candid Public, would be altogether improper; as such, I shall conclude this address with the addition only of one observation;—that though conquered by Mr. Humphreys in the battle at *Odiham*, I entertain a meaner opinion of his abilities as a Professional Boxer, than when I first met him on the stage.

I remain, Sir, your's [*sic*],
DANIEL Mendoza.

No. 9, White-Street, Houndsditch,
Jan. 23, 17[8]8.

Source: *Whitehall Evening Post* (London), January 22–24, 1788.

DOCUMENT 1.12. HUMPHRIES'S LETTER TO THE EDITOR, JANUARY 24, 1788

Sir,

I ENTIRELY agree with Mr. Mendoza, "That it is highly improper to intrude farther on the indulgence of a candid public"—and, therefore, it is my determination, not to enter into the particulars of his last letter, though replete with evasion, absurdity, and falsehood.—Thus much I do venture to pronounce—tho' no Critic—a character which Mr. Mendoza has, in the opinion of every one, very unsuccessfully aimed at—Some fame as a Boxer, I flatter myself, I am entitled to—as such, and on the terms already proposed on my part, I am ready to meet him;—and with his immediate and unreserved acceptance or refusal of these terms, shall end our literary intercourse.

Mr. Mendoza says, "I am afraid of him"—The only favour I have to beg, is, that he, or any of his friends, will be kind enough to tell me so *personally*, and spare me the trouble of seeking them.

Jan. 24, 1788. RICHARD HUMPHREYS

Source: *Whitehall Evening Post* (London), January 24–26, 1788.

DOCUMENT 1.13. MENDOZA'S LETTER TO THE EDITOR, JANUARY 27, 1788

SIR,

TO prevent the tedious necessity of a reference to the several letters which I have written, and which have appeared in your Paper; I am induced to take my leave of the Public, with the insertion once more of the Conditions of my Challenge to Mr. *Humphreys;* and I beg that the world will consider them, as open to the acceptance of that Gentleman, whenever he may think better of his *Boxing* abilities.

The first condition is, that I will fight him for 250 guineas a side;—the second, the victor to have the door;—third, the man who first closes to be the loser;—fourth and last, the time of fighting to be in the October New-market Meeting.

Mr. Humphreys would do well to insert this challenge in his memorandum book; and as a teacher in the art of boxing, it would not be amiss to have it well penned, neatly framed, and hung up in his *truly Scientific Academy.*

I remain, Sir, your humble servant,
DANIEL MENDOZA

No. 9, White-street, Houndsditch,
Jan. 27, 1788.

Source: *Whitehall Evening Post* (London), January 26–29, 1788.

DOCUMENT 1.14. JAMES GILLRAY'S DEPICTION OF THE ODIHAM MATCH

The caption reads: "Foul Play, or Humphreys and Johnson a Match for Mendoza. Dedicated to Wilson Braddyl Esqr. Gymnastico Generalissimo. This extraordinary Match was Fought at Odiham in Hampshire Jany. 9th 1788, after 25 Minutes Contest, Mendoza by his superior Skill carrying off the Honors of the day from his Antagonist, when Johnson after having recovered Humphries (who was nearly deprived of Life from a Knock-down Blow) by pouring cold water on his Stomach, finding him still weak & staggering from another blow, & Mendoza aiming another which must have decided the Battle very Judiciously [sic] steped [sic] in between, & by his address entirely chang'd the Scene; in consequence of which, several Gentlemen (who did not wish to gain by collusion) withdrew their Betts. Humphrey [sic] relying on such another Step, has thought proper to accept Mendoza's Challenge for another Combat, but like a bold Briton! has proposed such terms, as he knows his antagonist cannot possibly comply with from the state of his finances!!!—"I have done the Jew!" . . . [illegible] Humphries Letter to Braddyl.'"

Source: © National Portrait Gallery, London.

DOCUMENT 1.15. MENDOZA'S ACCOUNT OF THE ODIHAM MATCH, EXCERPTED FROM HIS MEMOIRS (PUBLISHED 1816)

On the 9th of January 1788, this contest took place, according to appointment, at Odiham, a stage having been erected for that purpose in an inn yard, which was speedily filled with spectators, who paid half a guinea each for admission. On this occasion Tom Johnson and Tom Tring were my opponent's second and bottle holder; and two men of the names of Jacobs and Isaacs were mine: Mr. Ford and Mr. Moravia were umpires; the former chosen by my opponent, and the latter by myself.

At the commencement of the contest, the bets were three to two against me, but after a few rounds, there was a material variation, as I evidently then possessed the superiority; and at the end of twenty minutes, the odds were five to two in my favour; notwithstanding which however, Mr. Humphreys had the good fortune to come off victorious, the reasons for which I shall now explain.

It was expressly agreed between my opponent and myself, previous to the contest taking place, that there should be only half a minute allowed between each round, notwithstanding which at one time, when nearly exhausted, he complained of the tightness of his shoes, and was forty seconds beyond his time in changing them for a pair of socks, yet no advantage was taken or attempted to be taken on my part of this circumstance. Afterwards, at a very critical period of the battle, I aimed a blow which, in all probability would have proved decisive, had not Johnson unfairly caught the same, and thereby deprived me of a very favourable chance of gaining the victory: this caused some little altercation at the moment, but passed on as my umpire yielded to the opinion of my opponent's friends, who offered some frivolous excuse in vindication.[1]

Notwithstanding these disadvantages however, I felt in high spirits, and was highly gratified with the idea of surmounting every difficulty, and thereby gaining greater honour, and therefore set-to again with ardour, when in endeavouring to throw my opponent, he seized the rails surrounding the stage and maintained his hold, with such firmness, that I could not effect my purpose; and being off my balance, he was easily enabled to pitch me on my head, which nearly decided the battle against me. I fought however two more rounds, but in the last received a fall that completely terminated the contest, for the excruciating pain I now felt in my loins rendered me unable to stand; consequently Mr. Humphreys was declared the victor, after a severe contest of forty-seven minutes.

---

[1]Mendoza wrote the following in a footnote: "The conduct of my umpire appeared very extraordinary at the time; but I afterwards learnt he had laid money against me, consequently he could not be expected to be very willing to decide against himself!"

Source: *Memoirs of the Life of Daniel Mendoza; Containing a Faithful Narrative of the Various Vicissitudes of his Life, and an Account of the Numerous Contests in which he has been Engaged, with Observations on Each; Comprising also Genuine Anecdotes of many Distinguished Characters, to which are Added, Observations on the Art of Pugilism; Rules to be Observed with Regard to Training, &c.* (London, 1816), 82–85.

SECTION 2. SOURCES ON THE STILTON MATCH
DOCUMENT 2.1. THE AGREEMENT

The battle between Humphreys and Mendoza takes place, as has been before stated, at Stilton this day.

This contest, as well as that which took place between the two combatants, at Odiham, is expected to prove one of the most scientifick that has been exhibited for many years past, as both the boxers pride themselves on their superior *skill* and *dexterity* over the rest of their profession.

The principles on which the battle will be conducted are,

1. That if either of the combatants falls without receiving a blow, he loses the battle, unless such fall should be deemed by the umpires accidental.
2. No person to be admitted within the place of fighting but the umpires and seconds; and
3. Both the seconds on the setting to of the parties shall retire to the separate corners of the enclosure.

These are the three essential articles formally agreed between them and committed to writing relative to the battle.

Humphreys has for his second that veteran in the art, his old friend Johnson; and Mendoza, Capt. Brown, an amateur of the science.

Twelve hundred tickets have been printed, (and not fifteen hundred as has been asserted,) one half of which are to be disposed of by Humphreys, and the other half by Mendoza. Half a guinea we believe is the price of each.

Source: *Gazetteer and New Daily Advertiser* (London), Wednesday, May 6, 1789.

DOCUMENT 2.2. A REPORT IN *DIARY OR WOODFALL'S REGISTER*

HUMPHREYS AND MENDOZA.

(Received by Express from STILTON *at* THREE *o'Clock This Morning.)*

The long expected battle between Humphreys and Mendoza yesterday took place at Stilton. A spacious amphitheater was erected for the purpose of seeing this contest in the Park of Mr. Thornton. It consisted of an erection of seats round a space of forty eight feet in circumference, raised one above another, and capable of holding between two and three thousand persons. About that number of spectators were present, the highest seat was removed at the distance of eighteen feet from the ground, and every man could see the combat clearly and distinctly.

Between one and two o'clock, Humphreys appeared on the turf, accompanied with Johnson as his Second, and a person, whose name we did not learn, as his Bottle-holder, and Mr. Coombs as his Umpire. Mendoza soon afterwards entered the field of action, attended by his Second, Captain Brown, his Bottle-holder Ryan, and his Umpire Sir Thomas Apryce. They stripped, and on setting-to, the seconds retired to the separate corners of the inclosure, according to the previous agreement of both parties.

Humphreys first struck at his antagonist in the face. The blow was stopped, and Mendoza *returned* with great quickness, and knocked him down. The second and third rounds were terminated in exactly the same manner. And after a contest for about forty minutes, in which Mendoza had evidently the advantage,—generally catching his adversary's blows on his arm and knocking him down or throwing him—a cessation was put to the battle by a circumstance which created much confusion among all parties.

In the *twenty-second* round Mendoza struck at Humphreys, on which the latter dropped. As the articles of agreement specified, that he who fell without a blow should lose the battle, a general cry of "Foul! Foul!" took place, and Mendoza's friends declared that he had won it. All those interested, however, in the fate of Humphreys exclaimed, "that it was fair," and the whole was immediately a scene of uproar and confusion. Humphreys, as well as Johnson, and part of the spectators, insisted that the blow was stopped before he fell; the partisans of the other side were as vehement in avowing a contrary declaration. The matter, however, could not be decided, as the Umpire of Mendoza declared it foul, while that of his adversary declined giving his opinion on the subject. Captain Brown told Johnson that he was a liar and a blackguard; this assertion was answered by the other walking up to him with a stern and menacing look; and it was a matter of dispute, whether a bye-battle would not have taken place between the seconds.

Humphreys came several times to his antagonist, and called on him to fight out the battle, but this Mendoza's friends would not suffer, on which Humphreys threw up his hat and challenged him to the contest. A number of people exclaimed, that this went nothing towards deciding the point in dispute; and the battle would perhaps have been a drawn one had not Mendoza, either advised by his friends, or irritated at his adversary's coming so often across the ring, and taunting him with not continuing to fight, consented to resume the contest. On this they again set to, and the two first rounds were terminated by Mendoza knocking down his antagonist. They fought for about half an hour, during which time Mendoza seemed evidently to have the advantage; and at last gained the battle by a violation, on the part of his antagonist, of the articles of agreement. After some blows had passed in the last round, and Humphreys had given way, Mendoza followed him up, and was preparing to strike, on which Humphreys fell, and as it was obviously without receiving the blow, he was universally declared to have lost the battle.

With regard to skill in the conduct of this boxing-match, Mendoza appeared evidently to have the superiority. His antagonist suffered him to gain ground upon him during the whole of the contest, and generally flinched, whenever he appeared ready to make a blow. Mendoza, on the contrary, stood up to him with great manliness and followed him with a coolness and resolution, which perhaps is more serviceable than the ardour and impetuosity of spirit, that distinguished his conduct at the battle of Odiham. Several times when Humphreys fell or was knocked down, Mendoza likewise pointed to him, and with an expressive countenance seemed to signify to the spectators the same sentiments.

When Humphreys closed likewise, he said several times to Mendoza "very well indeed! Very well!" on which Mendoza, when he threw him, repeated his words, and patted him with an air of mockery.

The only blows of considerable consequence which Mendoza received, was one on the cheek, and several in the back, at the time that they were in act of closing. Humphreys, towards the conclusion of the battle, made several very neat darts at the pit of his adversary's stomach, which Mendoza stopped incomparably well. They must, had they taken place, have proved inevitably fatal.

Humphreys was much beaten about the face. One eye was closed up, and his forehead cut above the other; his lip likewise was cut, and he was observed several times to spit blood.

It is somewhat singular that during the battle of Humphreys and Mendoza, notwithstanding the advantages which the latter appeared to possess, the betts continued invariably in favour of the former.

Whatever impressions this account may give of the conduct of Mendoza, it is nothing but an impartial statement of facts; and Humphreys himself, if actuated by his well known liberality, will allow that his adversary fought with wonderful science and intrepidity.

Source: *Diary or Woodfall's Register* (London), Thursday, May 7, 1789.

DOCUMENT 2.3. A REPORT IN THE *GENERAL EVENING POST*

Captain Brown was the second to Mendoza,—Johnson to Humphreys.

The parties set to about ten minutes after one, and after the fight had continued for about forty minutes, a dispute arising concerning a *shift* or *drop,* Mendoza insisted, that according to the articles of the battle, he had fairly won; particularly as Humphreys had once or twice before, early in the battle, *dropped* without being knocked down.

The Umpire of Mendoza was of the same opinion, and declared it foul, while that of his adversary declined giving his opinion on the subject. Captain Brown told Johnson that he was a liar and a blackguard: this assertion was answered by the other walking up to him with a stern and menacing look; and it was a matter of dispute whether a bye-battle would not have taken place between the seconds.

The altercation lasted near an hour, when Mendoza consented to renew the battle, and the combatants once more set to; but it was only to display the superior and decisive skill of Mendoza, who in about half an hour so completely dressed his antagonist, by repeated knock-down blows, that Humphreys, whose proud spirit could not submit to say he had got enough, evidently and palpably fell back without being touched.

This determined the day, it being considered as the signal or acknowledgment that he could hold out no longer.

Had Humphreys stood to his man, it was thought Mendoza would not have any great cause to rejoice in his victory; he fought on the retreat, and Mendoza never failed to drive him on the rails of the stage, where he almost constantly knocked down his man, to the great mortification of the knowing ones, who were all completely taken in; the bets being seven to four, six to four, five to four, two to one, and an hundred to forty on Humphreys.

In justice, however, to the parties, it must be confessed, that the favourite endured a most severe battle before he gave up; and that Mendoza never flinched from his man, but kept laughing at him, as if he had a school boy to deal with.

It is computed there were about 2000 spectators present, amongst whom were Lord Delaware, Lord Tyrconnel, Major Hanger, Mr. Braddyll, and several other celebrated amateurs of the science.

The celerity with which Mendoza struck his man, exceeds all description; and was so decisive in the end, that neither the superior strength and weight of Humphreys, nor the reach of his arm, could defend him from the lightning of Mendoza's wrist.

A carrier-pigeon was sent off with the intelligence to Duke's Place; and it was somewhat remarkable, that not above two or three of the tribe of

Abraham were observed to bear testimony to the victory of their brother of the beard.

Source: *General Evening Post* (London), May 7–9, 1789.

DOCUMENT 2.4. A REPORT IN THE *WHITEHALL EVENING POST*

HUMPHREYS AND MENDOZA.

Neither of the combatants were much hurt on Wednesday last. The eye of Humphreys was closed, and there was a cut over the other.

Mendoza received a very violent blow on the side of his head; and *stopped one blow* well, which might have terminated the contest.

When the first dispute took place, Mendoza was so distressed, that two and three to one were laid he did not renew the battle; and he was only forced to it by the company declaring that the door-money should all go to Humphreys, who offered to stake the whole of it on the battle going on.

The Amphitheatre was one of the finest spectacles that could well be exhibited. It was to contain about 2,500 persons, and it was well filled. The accommodation of the latter seats were so good, that they were only twenty feet from the ring.

Half-a-crown in every half-guinea went to the man who built the Amphitheatre.

The sums of money that were lost on the battle were immense. The door-money went two-thirds to the conqueror, one to the loser. Mendoza's gains are called 1000 [pounds].

The time of the first set-to was one o'clock, till forty-two minutes past. The dispute on the fall was not settled till seven minutes before three. At fifteen minutes past three the second set-to ended.

The Capt. Brown who seconded Mendoza, was formerly a Quarter Master in the Blues, and is the husband of Lady Ligonier, who, taking a fancy to his person, married him.

Source: *Whitehall Evening Post* (London), May 7–9, 1789.

DOCUMENT 2.5. A REPORT IN THE *MORNING POST AND DAILY ADVERTISER*

The following account of the contest between HUMPHREYS and MENDOZA, which took place on Wednesday last at STILTON, may differ from other representations of this engagement, but we derive it from a very respectable authority, that is ready to vouch for its truth and impartiality.

A large octagonal theatre was the scene of action. MR. LEVERTON the Surveyor, being on the spot, thought it a duty of humanity to examine into its strength; and this Gentleman not conceiving it capable of supporting the number of spectators who might be expected to occupy it, it was properly strengthened.

A very large concourse of people were present and the theatre was so commodiously designed, that all the spectators had a full view of the whole.

A little after one o'clock HUMPHREYS came into the ring, accompanied by Mr. Harvy COOMBE, his *umpire*, JOHNSON his *second*, and MR. FORD. In a few minutes after Mendoza entered, attended by Sir Thomas APPRICE, his *umpire*, CAPT. BROWN, his *second*, and RYAN.

After the usual ceremony of shaking hands, the combatants *set-to*: at this time the *odds* were *seven* to *four*, and *ten* to *five* in favour of HUMPHREYS.

For several rounds they fought at a *distance*, the *odds* remaining the same. HUMPHREYS then made a sharp assault, and knocking down his adversary, the odds were *three* to *two* on his side.

In a few rounds more HUMPHREYS fell, when Mendoza called out, he had "Won the money." The umpires being applied to, MR.COOMBE pronounced it *fair*, as HUMPHREYS having received a blow, in the stopping of which, he fell.

A contrary opinion was expressed by SIR THOMAS APPRICE, but the majority concurring in the opinion of HUMPHREYS'S Umpire, Sir Thomas prevailed upon Mendoza to renew the fight, upon the appointment of a third Umpire, and MR. HARVEY ASTON was chosen.

The fight was then renewed. At the first round HUMPHREYS seemed to have the advantage, and the betts were *two* to *one* in his favour, but owing to the steadiness and superior condition of Mendoza, (HUMPHREYS having for some time been unwell) the latter began to obtain the ascendancy, and at the end of fifteen or twenty minutes, HUMPHREYS fell without a blow, on which the Umpires unanimously decided in favour of Mendoza. Upon this, great acclamation arose, and Mendoza having been raised upon the shoulders of his friends, enjoyed the triumph of success. It is to be observed that till the moment before the last fall of HUMPHREYS, no *odds* were offered in favour of Mendoza.

Source: *Morning Post and Daily Advertiser* (London), Friday, May 8, 1789.

DOCUMENT 2.6. A REPORT IN THE *MORNING STAR*

In addition to our account of yesterday, copied into the other Prints, concerning the victory obtained by MENDOZA, we add the following particulars:

The Booth on which Mendoza and HUMPHRIES fought, was of an octagon form.

It held about sixteen hundred people.

Nearly, if not the whole of that number were present.

Each paid Half a Guinea for admission.

The battle began precisely at *one*.

HUMPHRIES was thrown four times in the first *six* minutes, although MENDOZA fought almost entirely on the *defensive*, as he continued to do for ten minutes longer.

MENDOZA then began to *attack* his antagonist, driving him from the centre of the ground to the railing, during which he generally made two or three blows.

HUMPHRIES always *fell* or *hugged* MENDOZA.

MENDOZA always contrived, in these falls, to get uppermost:

After fighting 39 minutes, SIR THOMAS APRICE, one of the Umpires, called out, that HUMPHRIES had fallen without any blow being struck at him. This, according to the Articles of Agreement, must have determined the battle in favour of MENDOZA.

But Mr. HARVEY COOMBE, the other Umpire, declared his opinion, that a BLOW *was* struck.

There being no other Umpire previously chosen but the above two, and the impropriety of choosing one then, when every one was interested, being so apparent, rendered an impartial decision impossible.

Here, notwithstanding, HUMPHRIES braved MENDOZA to renew the fight, and contrary, we believe, to the wishes of the *knowing ones*, who otherwise would have made it a drawn battle, MENDOZA, at the desire of SIR THOMAS APRICE, boldly renewed it.

The first blow at this second onset, MENDOZA struck HUMPHRIES under the left ear.

This apparently seemed to decide the battle. For HUMPHRIES, after reeling back on the railing, fell on his face.

In about fifteen minutes and an half HUMPHRIES fell, and was declared to do so without a blow.

This terminated the battle in favour of MENDOZA.

A Gentleman who was a minute spectator of the whole, took notice, that HUMPHRIES fell *forty-two* times, *nine* times of which MENDOZA fell under HUMPHRIES.

Source: *Morning Star* (London), Friday, May 8, 1789.

DOCUMENT 2.7. A REPORT IN THE *WORLD*

HUMPHRIES and MENDOZA.

THORNTON *Park, near Stilton.*

OF THIS CONTEST, were yesterday various accounts in town. We shall give, from letters now before us, an authentic and impartial one.

HUMPHRIES had *Johnson* for his Second; Mr. COOMBES was the Umpire on his part.

MENDOZA had *Quarter-Master* BROWN to his Second, SIR THOMAS APPRYCE was the Umpire on the part of the latter.

At the first *setting-to,* the odds were seven to four, and two to one upon HUMPHRIES, his state of health not being perfectly known. But the first blow he made, was caught by MENDOZA, and HUMPHRIES was in return knocked down.

In the course of the contest, he was knocked down sixteen different times.

After fighting *forty-two minutes,* HUMPHRIES, as was said, shifted; this caused a long contest on the part of the Seconds, and which terminated in an agreement to fight, between JOHNSON and BROWN.

That it was not done purposely, HUMPHRIES'S anxiety to bring on the contest again, was some proof. He did every thing to provoke MENDOZA to begin again.

MENDOZA was advised to do so—and after they had fought nearly *twenty minutes longer,* HUMPHRIES *shifted* without receiving a blow, and the battle was adjudged to MENDOZA.

MENDOZA fought scientifically and coolly:—HUMPHRIES with heat and impetuosity; and as if he wanted to bring the matter to a *short issue,* either from Betts about time, or from a consciousness that his health would not serve him for a long battle.

HUMPHRIES shewed great gallantry through the whole; and had *his health* been what it was formerly, would undoubtedly have been the conqueror. But in the science, and the lately acquired strength of his antagonist, he had *now* too powerful an adversary for a *Coup de Main.*

HUMPHRIES has lately had a *paralytic stroke;* and from which he has not, nor will recover but by time.

Neither of the *Combatants* were much hurt. The Eye of HUMPHRIES was closed, and there was a cut over the other.

MENDOZA received a very violent blow on the side of his head; and *stopped one blow* well, which might have terminated the contest.

When the first dispute took place, MENDOZA was so distressed, that two and three to one were laid, he did not renew the battle; and he was only forced to it by the company declaring, that the *Door-money* should all go to HUMPHRIES, who offered to stake the whole of it on the battle going on.

The AMPHITHEATRE was one of the finest spectacles that could well be exhibited. It was to contain about 2,500 persons, and it was well filled. The accommodation of the latter seats were so good, that they were only twenty feet from the Ring.

Half-a-Crown in every Half-Guinea went to the man who built the AMPHITHEATRE.

The sums of money that were lost on the battle, were immense. The DOOR MONEY went two-thirds to the Conqueror, one to the Loser. Mendoza's gains are 1000 [pounds].

The TIME of the first set-to, was one o'clock, till forty-two minutes past. The dispute on the fall was not settled till seven minutes before three. At fifteen minutes past three the second set-to ended.

Sir T. APPRYCE and MR.COOMBES both conducted themselves in the best style.

The SECONDS.—*Johnson* is well known—*Brown* is a fine made active fellow.

Source: *World* (London), Friday, May 8, 1789.

DOCUMENT 2.8. A REPORT IN *FELIX FARLEY'S BRISTOL JOURNAL*

Yesterday at One o'clock, the famous combatants Humphreys and Mendoza met at Stilton, and set to, fighting with various success for thirty five minutes, when Mendoza aimed a blow at Humphreys, which the latter evaded by falling,—Here a dispute arose whether the *fall* did not forfeit the battle; it being an express stipulation, that neither should drop without a *knock-down* blow.—Above half an hour was spent in altercation on this point.— To put an end to it, the friends of Mendoza advised him to set to again, which he readily consented to. After another quarter of an hour's fighting, in which Humphreys was considerably worsted, he made a second *fall,* and in so palpable a way, as to leave no room to doubt of its being a *shift.*—The victory of Mendoza was now decisive, and allowed on every side, so much so, that they who are not the foremost to pay their money without conviction, parted with it readily.—Humphreys fought the whole time with much warmth, and with great confidence of success; which the acclamations of a surrounding crowd seemed to inspire him with.—Mendoza was on the whole very calm, very collected—and bore the impetuous attacks of his antagonist with great courage.—From this possession of temper, and from much prior exercise, the issue of the battle turned as it did.—Brown was the second to Mendoza—Johnson to Humphreys.—A quarrel arose, whilst they were fighting, between the two seconds, about the fairness of a blow: they were going to decide it by dint of manhood, but the bye-standers interfered.—They have staked, however, ten pounds to fight at some distant period for a hundred guineas.—When the above battle was ended, Crab and the Tinman fought, on the same turf, for five and thirty minutes.—Crab was at last the victor.—Almost all the amateurs in town or country were present.—The betts, when Humphreys and Mendoza were put together a second time, were two to one in favour of the latter.

The Prince of Wales, much to his honour, peremptorily refused his countenance to the *pugilistic* exhibition at Stilton.

Source: *Felix Farley's Bristol Journal* (Bristol, England), Saturday, May 9, 1789.

DOCUMENT 2.9. A REPORT IN THE *PUBLIC ADVERTISER*

The battle between Humphries and Mendoza, in point of opposition, was not so obstinate as that at Odiham; but was obstinate enough to convince that it was in earnest.

Of the blows that were struck, Mendoza's were the most numerous; and it is doubted whether they were not the heaviest.

Humphries's object of assault was different from Mendoza's; the first aimed, for the most part, at the stomach; the last, at the head.

In catching blows, vast skill was discovered by Mendoza—and his return of the attack, almost on the instant of defence, shewed extraordinary agility.

In temper, Humphries was inferior.

His impetuosity at first weakened his after-efforts.

He endeavoured at a speedy victory—it was farther off than was imagined.

Considerable bets were depending, that the battle would be won by Humphries within twenty minutes.

Hence Mendoza's guard was so frequent in the early fighting. He acted solely on the defensive.

Of detriment received—no one has vast reason to complain.

Mendoza got a blow under the left eye, the impression of which will last some time; and two or three more on the ribs were all that he took.

Humphries's head was much bruised; one of his eyes, to use a technical phrase, was *sewed up,* and his upper lip cut nearly through.

Except such of the attendants at boxing matches as have died by the *rope,* we have not had a regular account of the death of more than *two* within the twelve months, who have quitted this world "in the labour of their vocation."—As many serious people, however, do not conceive that this savage and brutal behavior being suffered, tends much to dignify the country in the eyes of foreigners, or to polish or mend the morals of the lower class of people, and thereby render them good subjects and peaceable neighbours, they are not a little happy to hear it whispered that a motion will, in the course of the present or ensuing term, be made in the Court of King's Bench, for a Rule against the Magistrates of the County where a late boxing-match was, to their shame and disgrace, permitted to be decided, to shew cause why an information should not be granted. If this is true, it redounds not a little to the honour of our present Administration, as, to render a stream clear, the fountain-head should first be cleansed.

Source: *Public Advertiser* (London), Saturday, May 9, 1789.

DOCUMENT 2.10. HUMPHRIES'S LETTER TO THE EDITOR, MAY 11, 1789

SIR,

AS many reports have been circulated in consequence of the issue of the late engagement between myself and Mendoza, highly injurious to my character, and without the smallest foundation, I think it a duty to myself to offer some public vindication of my conduct, being conscious of having acted with the most honest endeavours to gratify the expectations of my friends, and the curiosity of the public. Prejudices of the kind which I allude to, are easily received into the minds of people who are rendered more susceptible of them by disappointment, but are always removed with great difficulty. Having, therefore, so arduous a task to perform, I fear I shall be under the necessity of trespassing longer than I could wish on the public attention, in giving a full detail of the most material circumstances which attended the battle: I shall, however, state them with so strict an observance of truth, as to compel an admission of them, from the most interested and partial friends of my opponent.

It will be unnecessary to give a minute account of the battle previous to that dispute to which I attribute the issue of the contest: it will be sufficient to declare, that uniformly from the beginning till that time, the odds were two to one in my favour.

After the battle had continued near half an hour, I attacked Mendoza with such exertion and success, as to produce a change sufficiently apparent to heighten the betts as far as three to one. It has since transpired, and the assertion I am now about to make will be supported by the testimony of many respectable persons who were witnesses to the declaration of Ryan, that Mendoza at that time whispered to his bottle-holder, that he was unable any longer to continue the engagement.—However, at the instance of Ryan, he was persuaded once more to meet me, at which time, as a last effort, he aimed a blow with all the strength he was then possessed of, which I receiving on my left arm at the very moment when I was in the act of stepping backwards, I unavoidably fell to the ground. Upon this Mendoza instantly undertook to decide the battle in his own favour, by withdrawing himself from the ring, and declaring the fall thus unavoidably occasioned, to be unfair. Sir Thomas Apprice, who was then present as Mendoza's umpire, threw up his hat as a signal of his concurrence. Upon this Mr. Coombe, who stood in the same relation to me as Sir Thomas did to Mendoza, went up to enquire what reason he assigned for thus endeavouring to assume the victory, at the same time declaring upon his honour, that he had seen the blow which had thus unavoidably occasioned my fall. Sir Thomas only declared that he had not seen it, but would not take upon himself to declare that such blow had not been received.—Thus far I thought the determination of the umpires was sufficiently decisive to have prevented any further protraction of the battle; yet notwithstanding I went up repeatedly to Mendoza, and challenged him to renew the contest, although the *time* for *setting to* again had been repeatedly *called* by my umpire; after I had advanced into the middle of the ring and thrown up my hat in token of defiance, as well as to mark my claim to the victory in consequence of his not obeying the summons of the umpire to appear, Mendoza still persisted in an obstinate refusal to meet me for the space of AN HOUR and A QUARTER.—At this time Mendoza was told, that unless he would come forward to the engagement, he should not be allowed any part of the money collected at the door, and was thus at length persuaded to meet me once more. At the time when this dispute arose I was in a profuse sweat, but being thus obliged to remain for so long a time inactive, the perspiration was checked, and I then felt the effects of a rheumatic complaint, with which, it is universally known, I had been last winter very severely afflicted, although I had so far recovered from it as entirely to remove all apprehension of feeling such consequences during the time of my continuing to perspire.

Under these disadvantages I was to meet a man again, who had enjoyed a long and uninterrupted series of good health, who could by no means feel the same inconvenience from such interruption, but who on the contrary had a manifest advantage in thus obtaining time sufficient to recover himself, in a great measure, from the effects of the blows which he had received.

After the renewal of the battle, and the further continuance of it for a considerable time, I made a blow at Mendoza, and in endeavouring to retreat from his return blow, I sunk down, without the power of recovering myself, which not being deemed by the umpires to be an accidental fall, the battle was decided against me. As I am very confident after a battle obtained against me under such circumstances as are here related, and after one decisive victory on my side, that the superiority is not on the part of my antagonist, I have this evening sent Mendoza the following challenge.

R. HUMPHREYS.

Bernard's Inn, May 11.

To Mr. MENDOZA

I HAVE stated to the Public the reasons which induced me to send you this Challenge, which I offer on the following terms.

1st. That you meet me at any time in October next that you will fix.

2dly. That there shall be no money collected at the door, in order to obviate any suspicion which may arise, that that was the object of our meeting.

3dly. You shall name the sum which you wish to fight for.

4thly. I leave the TERMS of our engagement to YOUR OWN APPOINTMENT.

R. HUMPHREYS.

Source: *Whitehall Evening Post* (London), May 9-12, 1789.

DOCUMENT 2.11. MENDOZA'S LETTER TO THE EDITOR, MAY 16, 1789

COPY *of a* LETTER *sent from*
MENDOZA *to* HUMPHREYS.

Mr. HUMPHREYS,

IT has not arisen from inattention, that I have delayed a reply to your Challenge, but solely to arrange my engagements in the manner that will best enable me to comply with your wishes.

I have made at Manchester, Liverpool, and other places, appointments to exhibit publicly, and to teach the art of Boxing, which take place the middle of June, and will necessarily detain me in the country for some months: I am under the necessity, therefore, of declining your offer to meet in October; but submit the following terms to your consideration.

1st, I will either meet you on any day within the *first week* of the month of *June next,* or on the 5th day of *May,* 1790.

2dly, I do not insist on a collection at the door:—but to obviate any idea that *that* is the object of our meeting, I propose that the money so collected, after defraying unavoidable expenses, shall be given to the poor of the parish where we fight.

3dly, I will fight you for *love*—or the same sum for which we fought at *Stilton.*

4thly, I will fight you on turf, inclosed in a circle of equal dimensions as at our last contest—a stand-up fight—the person falling without a blow, to lose the battle.

5thly, That both Seconds, at the setting-to of the parties, shall retire to the sides of the place enclosed. The place of fight, umpires, and other preliminary conditions, to be settled at a previous meeting of our respective friends.

I am,
Your very humble Servant.

No. 3, Paradise Row, Bethnal Green,
May 16, 1789.

Source: *Whitehall Evening Post* (London), May 16–19, 1789.

DOCUMENT 2.12. JAMES GILLRAY'S DEPICTION OF THE STILTON MATCH

The caption reads: "The Battle between Mendoza and HUMPHREY [*sic*], fought on Wednesday May 6th 1789 at Stilton in Huntingdonshire; which terminated in favor of Mendoza; who having by his superior skill foild [*sic*] Humphrey in every endeavor, for 35 Minutes, obligd [*sic*] him at last to have recourse to the cowardly method of Falling to avoid the blows, by which according to the agreement he forfeited the honor of the day. But Mendoza, with unequaled Spirit & liberality, scorning so cheap a victory, after giving Humphrey half an Hours [*sic*] respite, engag'd him afresh, & after a second contest of 15 Minutes, obliged him to yield the laurel to superior skill—the Christian Pugilist proving himself as inferior to the Jewish Hero as Dr. Priestley when oppos'd to the Rabbi David Levi."

Source: © National Portrait Gallery, London.

DOCUMENT 2.13. MENDOZA'S ACCOUNT OF THE STILTON MATCH, EXCERPTED FROM HIS MEMOIRS (PUBLISHED 1816)

Upon this occasion JOHNSON and FORD were Mr. HUMPHREYS'S seconds, and BROWN and RYAN were mine. Mr. COOMBES and Sir THOMAS A. PRICE [APREECE] were umpires; the former being nominated on the part of my antagonist, and the latter chosen by me.

Soon after one o'clock, Mr. HUMPHREYS and myself entered the inclosure, accompanied by our respective seconds and umpires, and in a few minutes set to; when both the seconds immediately retired to the boxes, assigned for that purpose, on each side of the ring, conformable to the agreement between us. Having fought for the space of forty minutes, my antagonist seemed quite exhausted, and I was evidently gaining considerable advantage over him; when, either from weakness or otherwise, he fell without a blow; this circumstance excited considerable tumult, the spectators very loudly expressed their indignation at the circumstance and required that the contest should be decided in my favour. My opponent's friends however would not so easily yield the matter; and on the umpires being called on for their decision, they were compelled to solicit the aid of a third person, Mr. HARVEY ASTON, who, after the subject had been discussed a considerable time, gave it as his opinion, that as the fall appeared unavoidable, no advantage ought to be taken of the circumstances, but that we should set to again, and decide the contest.

Though an interval of twenty minutes had elapsed, during this dispute, to the benefit of my antagonist more than myself, (for he was so completely overpowered when he fell, that he would not have been able to continue the contest many minutes longer, had we not been interrupted) I felt in high spirits, and was gratified with the idea of gaining a victory, which I considered would reflect the higher honour on me, on account of my not taking the advantage over him, which it was generally considered I was entitled to. We accordingly set to again, and having fought for ten minutes more, my opponent fell *again*, without a blow; but now his friends offered no further observations in his defence; and the battle was unanimously given in my favour.

The conduct of my opponent in falling twice without a blow, excited general surprise and dissatisfaction. On referring to the correspondence that took place between us, after our first contest, it will be seen that it was his proposal, that *I should be bound to stand up like a man;* and he even professed to impute my motive for objecting at first to be *bound* to this condition, to *cowardice,* and a disposition to shift from and evade his blows: what then must have been the feelings of the publick, when they beheld him adopt the very conduct himself, he pretended to apprehend his antagonist would be guilty of?

Source: *Memoirs of the Life of Daniel Mendoza,* 152–55.

SECTION 3. SOURCES ON THE DONCASTER MATCH
DOCUMENT 3.1. THE AGREEMENT

Humphreys and Mendoza, each attended by their respective friends, for the purpose of settling the agreement relative to their next battle, have had a meeting, and subscribed to the following terms:

1st, that they will fight on the 12th day of May next, between the hours of twelve and two, for the sum of 20 [pounds] each; that sum of 20 [pounds] each being deposited in the hands of a mutual friend.

2d, The parties agree to fight on a turf place containing 48 feet square. The place to be chosen by Daniel Mendoza, who engages to apprise Richard Humphreys of the place for fighting, one month previous to the battle.

3d, That when the parties shall set to, their seconds shall immediately retire to their places allotted, and not interfere during the round.

4th, That it shall be a fair stand-up battle, and if either party shall fall without receiving a blow from his antagonist, he shall be deemed to lose the battle, unless the fall arises from accident, which, and all matters of dispute arising during the battle, shall be decided by the arbitrators, and if any difference shall happen between the arbitrators, they shall choose an umpire to decide the same, whose decision shall be final.

5th, That there shall be an enclosed place for fighting, and the money collected, after paying all expences of stage or otherwise, be divided as follows: the half to the winner and the other half to the loser; and it is agreed that the loser shall, out of the proportion he is to receive, pay to the overseer of the parish where the battle shall be fought, 50 [pounds] for the poor; provided his proportion of the door-money shall amount to that sum. But if he shall not receive so much, then he shall pay only such sum as he shall actually receive.

Witness our hand

R. HUMPHREYS.

D. MENDOZA.

Source: *London Chronicle* (London), January 16–19, 1790.

DOCUMENT 3.2. A REPORT IN THE *GENERAL EVENING POST*

The long expected contest between Humphries and Mendoza was decided at Doncaster on Wednesday.

About ten o'clock Humphries came on the stage, with Ward and Jackson as his second and bottle-holder. Mendoza appeared soon after, with Johnson and Butcher.

The Duke of Hamilton and Sir Thomas Appreece were umpires and they appointed Mr. Aston referee, in case of dispute.

At twenty minutes past ten the combatants set to; the odds six to four in favour of Mendoza.

Humphries approached his antagonist with great spirit; and, in the first round, at the conclusion of which he knocked Mendoza down, and fell upon him, shewed so evident a superiority, that the odds changed to five to four in his favour.

In the second round, Mendoza being unable to defend himself in any other manner, closed, and both fell; but Humphries sprained his knee so violently, that it was supposed he could not stand up to continue the fight, and the odds instantly changed to twenty to one against him.

Although so completely deprived of the use of one leg, as to fall whenever he attempted to lean on it—and, hopeless of winning, he maintained the contest with unconquerable obstinacy, for more than an hour, during which he was allowed, by all the fighting men, to have shewn more game, and stood a severer beating than any they had ever seen. The remonstrances of his friends being still ineffectual, his second and bottle holder were obliged to yield the battle for him.

We have not heard what sums were depending: but from the issue of the battle appearing so early to be clearly decided, it is probable that much was not won or lost.

Some conversation passed between Johnson and Big Ben. Ben contended for a stage of sixteen feet, alledging, that having witnessed Johnson's agility in running away from Perrins, he will not have the trouble of running after him. Johnson refuses to fight, but on a stage of twenty-four feet.— Thus stands the matter at present.

Source: *General Evening Post* (London), September 30–October 2, 1790.

DOCUMENT 3.3. A REPORT IN THE *LONDON CHRONICLE*

BOXING.

MENDOZA *and* HUMPHRIES.

THE final meeting between these two pugilists took place on Wednesday at Doncaster. More than 500 tickets, at half-a-guinea each, were issued on the occasion; and the spot fixed on for the contest was an inn-yard, bounded on one side by the backs of houses, and on the other by a strong paling, behind which ran a river; advantages that rendered it extremely difficult for any rabble, however powerful or numerous, to force their way into the inclosure.

The company having been admitted, and the spectators taken their seats in the benches which were erected contiguous to the stage, in three different parts of the yard, Humphries, and shortly afterwards, Mendoza, appeared, with their respective seconds, bottle-holders, and umpires. Humphries mounted the stage, which was about four feet high and 24 square, in great spirits and with wonderful activity, and Mendoza seemed equally free from any degree of apprehension. On stripping, it is remarkable, that Mendoza appeared the largest and heaviest man; a circumstance arising partly from his increase in bulk, and partly from the mode of training adopted by Humphries, apparently more for the purpose of rendering him light and active, than of adding to his weight.

The odds on stripping were five to four on Mendoza, and they were readily accepted, the friends of his antagonist being extremely sanguine, and seeming to entertain an idea that, as it would be impossible to beat the Jew if blows were watched for, and the fight carried on in a regular scientific manner, Humphries would begin with violence, and, overpowering his antagonist with impetuous exertions, would frustrate all his arts of defence, and speedily obtain the victory. This, after the past experience of Mendoza's skill, was certainly judicious, and appeared to have been the intention and hope of Humphries, since his onset was bold, rapid, and vigorous, which was repelled with equal force on the other side; and, after mutually closing, they both struggled, and fell. During the second round, they fought with the same spirit, and, of the two, Humphries struck more blows, without overpowering his antagonist. The third set-to was of long duration; both parties seemed cautious of giving or receiving a blow; but what was given or received was in Mendoza's favour, for he terminated the round by knocking Humphries down. They engaged again for some moments in much the same manner; but on the fifth set-to, the Christian having aimed a blow at the Jew's stomach, which Mendoza stopped, struck him in the face, when the hit was returned, and Humphries fell. After this a great number of rounds took place, and in almost all of them Mendoza had evidently the advantage, and Humphries generally dropped, sometimes from an ineffectual effort in closing, and sometimes not so much by the force of the stroke, as from that policy which is often used in boxing. Though evidently worsted almost throughout the battle, he occasionally fought with great resolution, and stood up a long time to his antagonist after one eye was closed, his cheek cut open, and several other severe blows had been received. He even, when persuaded by his friends to *give in*, requested them to suffer him to box a little more; 'for,' said he, 'the day is still long, and though the contest is entirely in Mendoza's favour, some chance blow may take place, or some accident unexpectedly happen, that may change the event of the battle.' This circumstance, however, was totally improbable; for his adversary was as fresh, and fought as well, at the end of the battle as at the beginning; whereas Humphries was wearied with his exertions, and if he had continued the combat would soon have been unable to see any object, in consequence of the blows which his antagonist had effectually put in. Indeed, it was not before the severe beating he had received rendered it impossible to stand up any longer without suffering still greater injury, that Humphries gave in, and the *battle was decided in Mendoza's favour.*

With regard to Mendoza, his behavior throughout the contest was both manly and generous. He fought from the beginning to the end of the battle extremely well. Several times when, in the act of closing, Humphries was about to fall, he prevented him by holding him round the neck with one hand, and lifting the other in the air for some moments, proved to his antagonist and the spectators what he had it in his power to do—when, instead of striking the decisive blow, he let him down gently and carefully, without the least hurt, to the ground.

Humphries for the most part struck round, and attempted to plant his blows with great judgment. He aimed chiefly at the temples, under the ears, on the ribs, and the stomach. Some of his strokes took place, but by far the greater part of them were stopped, in a capital style, by Mendoza. In the science of defence Humphries was certainly inferior; but he kept a long guard, and warded off several excellent hits in the middle and even towards the end of the battle. It was impossible for him, however, to prevent the quick motions of Mendoza, whose fist, (sometimes while Humphries was standing on guard, and sometimes while he was dealing his round blows at the head) flew, like lightning, in a strait direction betwixt his arms, and, at almost every stroke, cut him severely on the face. About the middle, and till the conclusion, of the contest, Mendoza repeatedly leaped up and striking strait over his guard hit Humphries several keen strokes, the effects of which were immediately evident. Humphries, likewise, often sprung forward with the same intention, but without similar success.

Mendoza was considerably cut between the right eye and the temple, and on the left ear. His head, likewise, was greatly swelled, and he received a gash upon his right ribs in consequence of a strait forward left-handed blow of his antagonist at his body. Humphries had several hits, which drew blood, under his left arm. His right eye was closed, and he received a severe wound over his left. His right check, and the left side of his nose, was cut as if with a razor by one of Mendoza's springing, strait blows; his upper lip was by the same stroke split, and when he attempted to wash his mouth, while on his second's knee, with water, the liquor mixed with the blood gushed through the incision. In closing fights, Mendoza had the advantage, as he generally was quick enough to introduce his arm between Humphries and himself, and struck the short blows necessary, in that situation, with more facility than his antagonist.

In the second round, Humphries sprained his knee so violently, that it was supposed he could not stand up to continue the fight, and the odds instantly changed to twenty to one against him. Although so completely deprived of the use of one leg, as to fall whenever he attempted to lean on it, and, hopeless of winning, he maintained the contest with unconquerable obstinacy for more than an hour, during which he was allowed, by all the fighting men, to have shewn more game, and stood a severer beating than any they had ever seen. The remonstrances of his friends being still ineffectual, his second and bottle-holder were obliged to yield the battle for him.

After the battle was over, Mendoza went up and shook his antagonist cordially by the hand; when addressing himself to the spectators, he thanked them for the partiality which he had always experienced from them, but declared that having engaged in this final contest with Mr. Humphries, he should never fight again.

Humphries was then carried through the crowd on the shoulders of his friends, and to avoid the disturbance of the place, so improper for any person in his situation, conveyed in a post-chaise out of the town. Mendoza was well enough to walk afterwards on the race ground.

The battle began about half past ten, and lasted an hour and four minutes. In the course of about twenty minutes the odds were forty to five, and ten to one in favour of Mendoza, and as the battle drew to a conclusion they rose higher.

Humphries had Ward for his second, Jackson for his bottle holder, and Harvey Aston for his umpire. Mendoza, for his second and bottle holder, Johnson and Butcher; and for his umpire, Sir Thomas Aprice. The Duke of Hamilton acted as third umpire to refer to in case of any difference that might arise between the two former.

After this contest some more business of the same kind took place, between a brace of young bruisers.

After the above fight, another, between Packer and Mendoza's cousin, took place—Great game was shewn by both these pugilists. Packer seemed to have benefited more by the instructions of Mendoza than his own relation had, and consequently he quitted the stage victorious. A collection was made for them.

The Ruffian and a Miller, who we understand is of Doncaster, were to have fought yesterday.

Big Ben publicly challenged Johnson, and wished to fight him. A dispute was the occasion; Johnson wanting the whole of the door-money to go to the victor, and Ben insisted that it should be equally divided. It was at length agreed, these heroes should fight in three months, for one hundred pounds.

Source: *London Chronicle* (London), September 30–October 2, 1790.

DOCUMENT 3.4. A REPORT IN THE *WHITEHALL EVENING POST*

BOXING.

This brutal custom being still suffered to disgrace the Nation, we have again permitted our Paper to be stained by the mention of a Boxing-match, in the sincere hope that it will meet the eye of those in whose power it is to punish the magistrates for so gross a neglect of their duty, in allowing the law to be wantonly violated by blackguards who are a dishonour to human nature.

MENDOZA and HUMPHRIES.

These two very celebrated Pugilists met on Wednesday last at Doncaster, to settle what the *knowing ones* call the *rubber,* or the odd game, they having won a battle each before.

The seconds on this occasion changed sides, Johnson being on the part of Mendoza, and Ward for Humphries.

Upon *setting to,* the odds were two to one in favour of the *Jew.* Humphries however gave the three first knock-down blows, and sallied so vigourously in the subsequent rounds, that the *Jews* began to hedge, and the odds became six to four in favour of Humphries.

The grand object of Humphries was evidently to exercise all his vigour in the outset, and gain the battle by rallying, without admitting the finesse of his adversary to come into play.

Of this Mendoza was perfectly aware, and fought solely on the defensive, but never fell without a knock-down blow. At one time, when both parties fell, Humphries appeared to have received a hurt in the knee, which, as he continued to exert himself, became of course still worse. Here the *Jew,* recovering on this second wind, became, in his turn, the assailant, and pushed his opponent with such successful vigour, that after fighting an hour and a quarter, Humphries was obliged to give in.

There was afterwards some little altercation, in consequence of complaints made by the friends of Humphries, that he had received a foul blow; but this did not last long, and it was finally determined that the battle had been fairly won.

Twenty-five guineas a side was the sum Humphries and Mendoza are said to have fought for.

After the conclusion of the battle, Mendoza thanked the spectators (who by the bye were very numerous) and assured them that he never would fight in public again.

At the door, upwards of 400 [pounds] were collected.

The Umpires were Col. Hamilton, Mr. Ford, and Mr. Harvey Aston, by whom any dispute between the former was to be decided.

After the above fight, another, between Packer and Mendoza's cousin, took place—great game was shewn by both these pugilists; Packer seemed to have benefited more by the instructions of Mendoza than his relation had, and consequently he quitted the stage victorious. A collection was made for them.

The *Ruffian* and a Miller, who we understand is from Doncaster, were to have fought yesterday.

Big Ben publicly challenged Johnson, and wished to fight him. A dispute was the occasion; Johnson wanting the whole of the door-money to go to the victor, and Ben insisting that it should be equally divided. It was at length agreed these heroes should fight in three months, for 100 [pounds].

Source: *Whitehall Evening Post* (London), September 30–October 2, 1790.

DOCUMENT 3.5. A REPORT IN THE *WORLD*

PUGILISM.

BY *EXPRESS* FROM *DONCASTER.*

The *Amateurs* of this *Polite Art* have crowded Doncaster, so that with Boxers and Jockies, scarce a bed is to be had in the whole place.

The former were highly gratified by the sport of Tuesday, on which day, at half after ten o'clock, HUMPHRIES and Mendoza appeared on the stage erected for them here.

They set to with great spirit, when the bets were seven to four on the Jew. HUMPHRIES rushed on his antagonist, and gave him the first knock down blow, by striking him on the belly, which cut him: the second round was a very excellent one, but HUMPHRIES closed, and by a fall sprained his knee. This accident, it was very evident, he never recovered through the whole of the fight, which otherwise might have lasted longer, but must have terminated as it did.

After these, they had SEVENTY rounds, when the superior art of Mendoza was so evident, that ten and fifteen to one were laid on him.

These rounds, though fatal to HUMPHRIES, did not lessen his spirit, of which he gave such proof as gained him the reiterated applause of the spectators. Mendoza, almost every blow he made, struck between his antagonist's guard, until, by repeatedly striking him in the face he had beat his nose to a jelly, and at every blow blood flew from his cheeks.

For some time before the conclusion of the battle, it was the wish of every one that HUMPRHIES should give in. Mendoza saw himself victor, and behaved in a manner that did him credit: he had such advantage, that he might have struck HUMPHRIES every time he came within the length of his arm, but he nearly raised him with his left arm, and gently laid him down with his right.

HUMPHRIES was again requested by his Second and the Umpires, to give up the fight, but he replied 'the day was not yet so far advanced, but that he might still be victorious.' He fought some time after this, but at length by the earnest entreaties, both of his friends and the adverse party, he gave up the contest.

There was not a man present but applauded him; even those that lost most by the event, were eager to praise him.

Mendoza was not hurt, except in the left arm, which was much beaten by stopping the blows of his opponent. After the fight, he got into a carriage, and went to the race-ground.— He was so elated with his victory, that he jumped round the stage, and hugged every man he came near, but particularly Sir THOMAS APREECE.

After the conclusion of the battle, Mendoza thanked the spectators, (who by the bye were very numerous) and assured them that he would never fight in public again.

At the door, upwards of 400l. were collected.

The Umpires were Col. HAMILTON, Mr. FORD, and Mr. HARVEY ASTON, by whom any dispute between the former was to be decided.

Mendoza's Second was JOHNSON—his Bottle-holder was BUTCHER.

HUMPHRIES was seconded by WM. WARD, and his Bottle-holder was JACKSON.

Twenty-five Guineas a side was the sum HUMPHRIES and Mendoza are said to have fought for.

After the above fight, another, between PACKER and Mendoza's Cousin, took place—Great game was shewn by both these Pugilists; PACKER seemed to have benefited more by the instructions of Mendoza than his relation had, and consequently he quitted the stage victorious. A collection was made for them.

The *Ruffian* and a *Miller*, who we understand is of Doncaster, were to have fought yesterday.

BIG BEN publicly challenged JOHNSON, and wished to fight him. A dispute was the occasion; JOHNSON wanting the whole of the door money to go to the Victor, and BEN insisted that it should be equally divided. It was at length agreed, these heroes should fight in three months, for 100l.

Source: *World* (London), Friday, October 1, 1790.

DOCUMENT 3.6. AN EXCERPT FROM A REPORT IN *ARGUS*

One of the *amateurs* present at the above battle, speaks with great rapture of Mendoza's superior generosity, as well as superior skill. Though Humphries had the advantage at the onset, yet soon finding his own inferiority, he made some desperate attempts, and even risked his own life, by violently aiming at his antagonist's heart.

Mendoza, soon perceiving the intention of the hopeless Humphries, cried out, 'Gentlemen, I will shew more humanity to my once master.' He kept his word; for at one time when they closed, he had the head of Humphries under his arm, and might easily have then decided the battle; but he let him loose without a blow.

'Cowards are cruel, but the brave
Love mercy, and delight to save.'

The picture of Mendoza is, we hear, crowned with garlands in all the public-houses in and about *Duke's Place.*

Source: *Argus* (London), Saturday, October 2, 1790. Editor's Note: most of this article was copied from the report in the *World* newspaper (see Document 3.5), but the *Argus* article included additional material, excerpted here.

DOCUMENT 3.7. AN EXCERPT FROM A REPORT IN *DIARY OR WOODFALL'S REGISTER*

FARTHER PARTICULARS.

DONCASTER, perhaps, was never so full of company as on Wednesday last. In addition to the attraction of the races, many hundreds of persons attended merely in order to see the battle. All the people from the neighbouring parts of the county, particularly from Sheffield, were present, and the gate of the inclosure, after the admission of those who came in with half guinea tickets, having been opened, either for whoever had interest to enter gratuitously, or for such as paid a smaller price, the place appeared to contain, on the whole, no less than *two thousand people,* part of whom sat on the benches that were erected for the purpose and part stood upon the ground.

Humphries merits much praise for his conduct; and even those who had betted in his favour and lost their money, were satisfied that he had done his best. But the report of his having dislocated his knee at the end of the second round, which was circulated by some persons, and stated in several of yesterday's papers, was extremely fallacious as well as injudicious; for the second round was over in less than five minutes, and Humphries fought an hour afterwards,— and that occasionally with great spirit—which would have been impossible had such an accident happened. The truth was that he hurt his knee at the time specified, but not so materially as to affect his conduct during the rest of the battle. The evil was no doubt magnified for the purpose of detracting from Mendoza's merit in gaining the victory.

During the contest, Jackson, one of the bottle-holders, addressed himself to Mendoza in a style of the lowest blackguardism. Sir Thomas Aprice reproving him for his conduct, and observing that no such language was used by any other party present, was answered in terms of some rudeness, on which the worthy Baronet replied with becoming spirit, that he would not suffer himself to be insulted, and that if Jackson said any thing more of the same kind, 'he would for once *reduce himself to his level,* and become a blackguard.' This manly declaration immediately drew an apology from Jackson, who said he was sorry if he had given Sir Thomas any offence.

Big Ben having challenged Johnson, was told from the stage, that he should have his desire the next morning, on condition that the door-money might all go to the winner. This Brian objected to; and Johnson agreed to fight with him on that day three months, and divide the door-money. Big Ben never looked fresher, nor in better condition.

After the battle, money was collected as a prize to be fought for by a cousin of Mendoza, and a young West-Country boxer of the name of Packer. Johnson seconded the Jew, and Ward the Christian. This was a most severe contest, for they fought at each other for almost an hour with much violence, and were both greatly bruised. On closing, they fell, when Aaron Mendoza being uppermost, Packer suddenly raised his knee, and canted him head over heels against the railing. The somerset was so severe, as to conclude the battle in Packer's favour.

With regard to the battle between MENDOZA and HUMPHRIES, the former fought so well, and the latter continued the contest with such perseverance, though severely beaten; they have both been so long at variance, exerted themselves so much for the satisfaction of their friends, and hazarded and borne such frequent marks of each other's violence; that it must be the wish of every person (especially of those who were present at their last battle) to see them henceforth united in the firmest friendship, and lost to the recollection of their former differences for-ever.

[In our Paper of Monday, we shall give a regular account of all the rounds in the first battle, of Wednesday last, as they were minuted-down at the time of their being fought.]

Source: *Diary or Woodfall's Register* (London), Saturday, October 2, 1790. Editor's Note: most of this article was copied from the report in the *London Chronicle* (see Document 3.3), but the *Diary or Woodfall's Register* article included additional material, excerpted here.

DOCUMENT 3.8. A REPORT IN *DIARY OR WOODFALL'S REGISTER* (PART 1)

BOXING.

HUMPHRIES *and* MENDOZA.

The battle between these two champions at DONCASTER, having been their concluding contest, set on foot with a view of determining on which side lay the superiority in the art of Boxing, we have inserted a more ample account of the business than is generally given to details of this nature. Maintaining a mode of conduct exactly opposite to that of some of the other daily papers, who have represented the whole affair with a most shameful partiality, the writer of the article in question has avoided every possible degree of bias or prejudice; and, in order still further to satisfy the publick curiosity, he concludes with a general statement of the various rounds, as they were regularly minuted down at the time of their being fought.

1. 1st Round. Sudden and violent. Both fell.
2. A rallying round again. Humphries struck Mendoza oftenest. They both received many blows.
3. Rather a long set-to, before any stroke was given. They were mutually cautious, and watched each other. Mendoza knocked Humphries down.
4. Mendoza struck Humphries in the face. Humphries returned. Mendoza knocked him down.
5. Humphries aimed a powerful blow at the stomach. Mendoza stopped it. Humphries hit Mendoza in the face. Mendoza returned it. Humphries fell.
6. Several smart blows. Humphries down.
7. Humphries aimed the first blow. Mendoza returned, and cut him down the cheek. Humphries fell.
8. Many blows on both sides. Humphries fell.
9. Humphries hit Mendoza on the side, and fell.
10. Humphries struck at Mendoza often in the face, and fell.
11. Humphries aimed a quick blow at the stomach. Mendoza stopped; struck in the face; and Humphries fell.
12. Humphries made a rush at Mendoza, and struck him in the face. Mendoza returned twice, and H. fell.
13. Mendoza struck H. in the face, and Humphries fell.
14. Closed. Humphries fell.
15. Humphries aimed at the stomach. Mendoza stopped. A smart round. Humphries fell.
16. Humphries struck at the face. Mendoza stopped, returned, and Humphries fell.
17. Humphries aimed at the face. Mendoza stopped, and was about to return, when Humphries fell. (Cry of *foul, foul!* in consequence of Humphries' dropping without a blow: succeeded by a cry of *fair, fair!*)
18. Mendoza aimed at Humphries' face. Humphries fell without a blow.
19. Mendoza struck H. over the breast. Humphries fell.
20. Mendoza struck Humphries in the face. Seemed to forget that he was not sparring, and hit him twice open-handed. Humphries fell.

21. Humphries sprung forward, and struck twice. Mendoza leaped backward, and out-reaching the violence of the blows, stopped them, turned, and Humphries fell.

22. Humphries aimed at the stomach; Mendoza stopped, returned, and Humphries fell.

23. Closing. Blows struck, in this awkward situation, by both. Humphries hit Mendoza in the face. Mendoza returned, and, in this close-fighting, Humphries fell.

24. Close-fighting; Humphries fell; Mendoza struck him before he was down.

25. Both struck many blows, in an instant, and closed. Struggled to throw each other. Mendoza threw Humphries.

26. An excellent round, sustained with rapidity and violence on both sides. Humphries fell.

27. Humphries struck. Mendoza stopped, and returned. Struck again, and Mendoza acted in the same manner. Humphries hit Mendoza, under, or upon the left ear, and fell.

28. Several blows by both. Humphries hit Mendoza, Mendoza returned, and Humphries fell.

29. Several blows. Humphries hit M. Mendoza returned, and Humphries fell.

30. Several blows. Humphries received a blow on the face, and fell.

31. Short round. Humphries struck Mendoza, and cut him near the right temple. Mendoza struck again, and Humphries fell.

32. Humphries struck. Mendoza stopped it, and struck again. Humphries fell.

33. Close-fighting. Mendoza struck short blows, and Humphries fell.

34. Several strokes. Mendoza hit Humphries a smart blow on the face, and Humphries fell.

35. Humphries sprung forward, and struck. Mendoza stopped, and Humphries fell, apparently without a blow.

36. Mendoza struck Humphries in the face. Followed it up by an under blow. Humphries fell.

37. Closed. Humphries grasped Mendoza with his right arm, and with his left struck under-blows at his body. Mendoza holding Humphries with his left, returned in the face, with his right hand; and Humphries being nearest the rails in this close contest, had his head hit against them, and fell.

38. Several ineffectual aims attempted, when Mendoza struck Humphries in the face, and Humphries fell.

39. Humphries struck often, Mendoza returned, retreating; and Humphries fell.

40. Humphries fought away *slap-bang*. Mendoza stopped all his blows, struck in return, and Humphries fell.
41. Closing-fight. Humphries gave way to the rails. A contest against them, and H. fell.

[*To be concluded to-morrow.*]

Source: *Diary or Woodfall's Register* (London), Monday, October 4, 1790.

DOCUMENT 3.9. A REPORT IN *DIARY OR WOODFALL'S REGISTER* (PART 2)

BOXING.
HUMPHRIES *and* MENDOZA. (ROUNDS CONCLUDED.)

42nd Round. Mendoza struck several blows, and Humphries fell.

43d. Closing towards the corner. Mendoza struck Humphries, and H. fell.

44. Humphries aimed, Mendoza stopped, returned twice, and Humphries fell.
45. Several blows struck by Humphries. Mendoza stopped them, struck again, and Humphries fell.
46. Mendoza struck over Humphries's guard at his face. Humphries returned, and, being about to fall, Mendoza struck an under blow, before he could accomplish his purpose. [Some hissing, succeeded by clapping.]
47. Several blows aimed, and stopped, on both sides. Mendoza struck Humphries twice on the ribs and Humphries fell.
48. Hits on both sides. Humphries closing, attempted to fall. Mendoza prevented him, by holding him round the neck with the left hand, and, lifting his right in the air for some moments, gently and carefully laid him on the ground, without striking a blow. [Much applause.]
49. Several blows attempted on both sides. Humphries kept striking round blows at his adversary's head. Mendoza aiming strait forward, between the opening thus made, hit Humphries on the face, and Humphries fell.
50. Mendoza made a spring, and struck Humphries by a strait forward blow, over his left eye. Humphries fell.
51. Mendoza sprung forward, and struck a strait blow over Humphries's mouth. Sprung forward again, and repeated the stroke. Humphries was much cut between the nose and upper lip.
52. Mendoza struck strait forward, and cut Humphries over the nose. Humphries bled much, and aimed a returning blow. Mendoza

stopped it, springing forward, cut him on the left eye, and Humphries fell.

54.[2] Mendoza struck strait forward, and cut Humphries's lip open. Humphries returned in vain. Mendoza ditto. Humphries struck many blows; Mendoza aimed between his guard, struck Humphries on the nose, and Humphries fell.

55. Mendoza sprung forward twice, struck Humphries both times on the face, and Humphries fell.

56. Humphries struck many round blows. Mendoza stopped them, and knocked him down.

57. Humphries aimed at Mendoza's stomach. Mendoza stopped. Humphries returned. Mendoza hit, and following him up knocked him down.

58. Many inconsiderable blows on both sides. Humphries fell.

59. Many blows. Humphries struck Mendoza on the face, and Mendoza fell.

60. Humphries sprung forward at Mendoza, and aimed at his face. Mendoza stopped, returned, and Humphries fell.

61. Humphries struck. Mendoza returned. Closed. Humphries was falling. Mendoza held him up, and for a few moments remained with his right hand uplifted; when instead of taking advantage of his situation, he lowered him carefully to the ground.

62. Some blows from Mendoza. Humphries fell.

63. Many hits. Mendoza struck. Humphries closed. Both attempted to strike, but Mendoza forcing his arm within gained an opportunity of hitting, and Humphries fell.

64. Mendoza struck at Humphries in the face. Humphries stopped. Mendoza caught hold of him to close, and Humphries fell.

65. Mendoza struck Humphries. Humphries attempted to return, but Mendoza got within his arms, and Humphries fell.

66. Humphries attempted to strike. Mendoza prevented the blow, by throwing out his left arm. Humphries tried again but ineffectually. Mendoza sprung forward, struck Humphries in the face, and knocked him down.

67. Many blows on both sides. Mendoza struck Humphries on the face, and Humphries fell.

68. Humphries attempted to strike. Mendoza stopped the blow, and hit him in the eye; so that the blood gushed forth, and Humphries fell.

---

[2]There is no number 53 in this account.

69. Humphries attempted to strike, but without much force. Mendoza stopped the blow. Both closed. Mendoza got his arm within, struck, and Humphries fell.
70. Many blows on both sides. Humphries seized Mendoza round the waist, and they both fell.
71. Mendoza tried to strike in the face. Humphries stopped. Mendoza aimed a blow at the stomach. Humphries stopped it. Mendoza hit [*sic*] in the face, and Humphries fell.
72. Mendoza struck a strait blow, with his right hand. Humphries stopped it. Mendoza sprung forward, and hit Humphries in the face. Humphries fell; and, giving in, the battle was declared in Mendoza's favour.

The circumstance of the last battle at Doncaster, having been fixed upon for the final decision of the differences between Humphries and Mendoza, induced the writer of this article to enter into a more ample account of their boxing match than he should otherwise have attempted, especially at a moment when contests of this nature are becoming extremely unpopular. The studied misrepresentations of some of the other papers, likewise, rendered it necessary for him to conclude with the preceding circumstantial detail of the several rounds, the perusal of which will give to those *amateurs* of pugilism, who were prevented by the distance of the place from attending the contest in question, a more perfect idea of the different mode of fighting of the two combatants than any general statement of the business could possibly afford. It will evidently appear that Mendoza chiefly relied on his skill in beating off the blows of his antagonist; and that Humphries depended for success on the vigorous modes of attack that he occasionally adopted, and when those failed on the more artful, but less manly, practice with which he so frequently terminated his rounds, of dropping. Humphries, however, it must be allowed, often fell merely in consequence of the blows he received, and of ineffectual attempts in closing. He fought infinitely better than in his former contest at Stilton, and proved wonderfully *game*. Mendoza seemed also much improved both in science and bulk; and behaved in several instances with commendable gallantry.

The blow which in a former account we mentioned Humphries so effectually to have made at the right ribs of his antagonist, has not been specified in the preceding detail, as the round in which it took place was not exactly observed, though it appears to have been inflicted in the early part of the battle.

Having said thus much we shall press the business no longer upon the public attention, but conclude by repeating our wish, that as the friends of Humphries during the last battle admired the spirit of the Jew, and those of Mendoza praised the perseverance and bottom of the Christian, and as those pugilists have decided their final contest, and done all that can be expected from them as enemies, they may, for the sake of novelty, try the effects of a firm and lasting friendship.

Source: *Diary or Woodfall's Register* (London), Tuesday, October 5, 1790.

DOCUMENT 3.10. JAMES GILLRAY'S DEPICTION OF THE DONCASTER MATCH

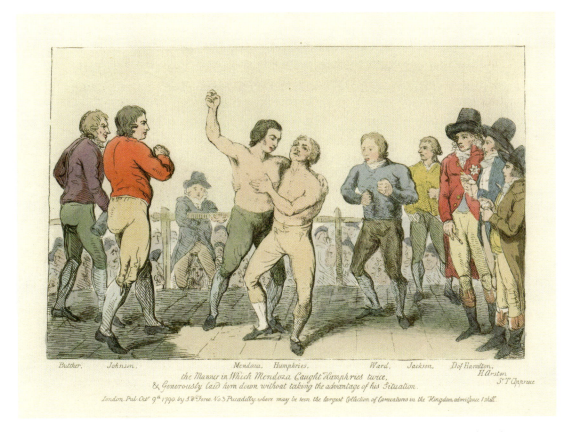

The caption reads: "the Manner in Which Mendoza Caught Humphries twice, & generously laid him down without taking the advantage of his Situation." The print also lists the figures from left to right (not counting the man climbing on the rail or any of the other spectators): Butler, Johnson, Mendoza, Humphries, Ward, Jackson, Hamilton, Aston, Apreece.

Source: Courtesy of The William A. Rosenthall Judaica Collection at the College of Charleston, in South Carolina.

DOCUMENT 3.11. MENDOZA'S ACCOUNT OF THE DONCASTER MATCH, EXCERPTED FROM HIS MEMOIRS (PUBLISHED 1816)

On this occasion, WARD and JACKSON were my opponent's seconds, and JOHNSON and BUTCHER were mine. Colonel HAMILTON and SIR THOMAS A. PRICE [APREECE], were umpires. Mr. HARVEY AS-TON was appointed third umpire, to refer to in case of any difference of opinion, that might happen to arise between the two former.

On stripping, it was observed, that I appeared the largest and heaviest man: this circumstance, which seemed to excite some surprise, arose partly from my increase in bulk, and partly from the mode of training adopted by my opponent, apparently more for the purpose of rendering him light and active than of adding to his weight.

On setting to, the odds were five to one in my favour, and they were readily accepted, as Mr. HUMPHREYS'S friends appeared extremely confident of his success, and seemed to entertain an idea, that though he would have little chance of success if blows were watched for, and the battle fought in a regular scientific manner; he might, by beginning with violence and overpowering me with impetuous exertion, frustrate all the arts of defence, and speedily obtain the victory.

Accordingly, the onset of my opponent was bold, rapid, and vigorous; but, in the course of twenty minutes, he became very much fatigued, and the odds were greatly against him; at length, after maintaining the contest for an hour and thirteen minutes, during which time we fought seventy-two rounds, he was completely exhausted, and giving in, the victory was declared in my favour.

Having made up my mind, previous to this last contest with Mr. HUM-PHREYS, that it should be the last pitched battle I would ever fight, I felt particularly anxious that our long contested claims to superiority, in the pugilistic art, should be fairly and finally decided, and was therefore determined that, in case of being victorious, his partisans should never have it in their power to assert, with truth, at any future opportunity, that my success ought to be attributed to superior circumstances, which chance had thrown in my way. On this account, I forbore to take many advantages which were in my power, and were fully authorized by the fairest rules of boxing. Among other opportunities that occurred, by which I might have put an end to the contest and have obtained the victory without further risk, had I been so inclined, it will suffice to mention that at three different times, I had my antagonist so completely in my power, that the battle might have been decided in an instant; these favourable opportunities occurred through his making ineffectual attempts at dropping, when by seizing him before he had effected his purpose, I was enabled to hold him in such a situation, that he could not have resisted a blow; and to convince him, as well as the spectators, of my being perfectly aware of what I had in my power, I held him in the situation with one hand and extended the other before him for the space of some seconds, when, instead of availing myself of these advantageous opportunities of terminating the contest, I laid him gently on the ground without the least injury.

At the termination of the contest, I shook my opponent by the hand, and addressing myself to the spectators, informed them, that having engaged in this final contest with Mr. HUMPHREYS, at his particular request, I had come to the determination to fight no more pitched battles.

Thus at length, the long disputed claims to superiority in the art of pugilism, between Mr. HUMPHREYS and myself, were by this third and last contest completely decided in my favour. I never afterwards received a challenge from him, or even heard of his professing the least inclination to engage with me a fourth time.

Source: *Memoirs of the Life of Daniel Mendoza*, 169–74.

PART III
HISTORICAL CONTEXT

You have now read the graphic history and (at least some of) the documents on which it was based. In this section (Part III) you will learn information designed to put what you have read into **historical context**. Deriving from the Latin word *contextus*, or "weaving together," context is surrounding information that enables us to give meaning to specific facts, and historical context is simply historical information that can shape our view of specific historical events or phenomena. For example, the meanings we can attribute to Mendoza's life and career will be different depending on the condition of Jews in eighteenth-century Britain and the attitudes of Gentiles (non-Jews) toward them. If the Jews were largely prosperous and respected at the time, we would interpret Mendoza's story differently than if they were mostly poor and subject to widespread prejudice. Thus it is important to examine the *context* of Jewish history and the history of Jewish-Gentile relations. Similarly, if few British people paid attention to sports, we would see the rivalry between Mendoza and Humphries in a different light than if sports were a major preoccupation at the time. Therefore it is important to examine the context of the history of sports. In what follows we will look at eighteenth-century Britain in the following contexts: (a) the history of the Jews, (b) anti-Semitism and tolerance in British society, (c) leisure, commerce, and the rise of spectator sports, (d) the history of boxing, (e) the role of nationalism, and (f) the role of gender. Don't worry if you are not familiar with all of these concepts; they will be explained shortly.

THE JEWS OF EIGHTEENTH-CENTURY BRITAIN

In the eighteenth century the Jewish community was relatively new to Britain. King Edward I had expelled the Jews from England in 1290, and it was only in 1656 that the "Lord Protector" Oliver Cromwell readmitted the Jews to what was then called the Commonwealth of England, Scotland, and Ireland. (We have seen from Chapter 1 of the graphic history that the Dutch Rabbi Menasseh Ben Israel had convinced Cromwell that the Jews would be useful to the economy and loyal subjects of the Commonwealth.

Cromwell may also have been influenced by the belief that admission of the Jews would hasten the Second Coming of Christ.)[1] At the beginning of the eighteenth century there were fewer than a thousand Jews in England.[2] By the time of Mendoza's birth (1765) that number had grown to about 8000. By 1800 there were between 15,000 and 26,000 Jews in Britain, the vast majority of whom lived in London.[3] Most of these lived in the poor neighborhoods of Aldgate parish (in the City of London) and Whitechapel (an East End suburb).

The Jewish population of Britain was divided into Sephardim and Ashkenazim. The Sephardim were descendants of those Jews who had been expelled from Spain and Portugal in the 1490s or had nominally converted to Christianity but practiced their religion in secret. Menasseh Ben Israel and the earliest Jewish immigrants to England were Sephardim. Generations

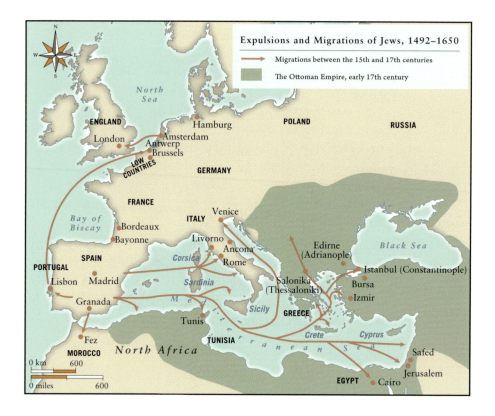

---

[1]On the religious reasons for Cromwell's for Cromwell's decision see David Katz, *Philo-Semitism and the Readmission of the Jews to England, 1603–1655* (Oxford, UK: Clarendon Press, 1982).

[2]I refer to "England" rather than "Britain" in 1700 because the Kingdom of Great Britain came into existence only in 1707, when the Kingdom of England, which included Wales, was joined to the Kingdom of Scotland.

[3]Todd M. Endelman, *The Jews of Georgian England, 1714–1837: Tradition and Change in a Liberal Society* (Philadelphia: Jewish Publication Society of America, 1979), 172–73.

of having to "fit in" had given the Sephardim special skills at assimilation, thus they quickly learned the language of the country in which they lived, dressed in the fashions of their new compatriots, and were hard if not impossible to distinguish from their non-Jewish neighbors. Many were lax in their observance of Jewish dietary laws and ate food that was not kosher. Although most of the Sephardic population was poor, an upper crust of bankers, financiers, and large-scale merchants gave the Sephardim an air of bourgeois respectability, at least in comparison to the Ashkenazim.

The Ashkenazim were originally from central and eastern Europe. Even poorer than the Sephardim, the Ashkenazim were also less assimilated. The native language of Ashkenazi immigrants was Yiddish, and many spoke only fragmented and heavily accented English. Generally more pious than their Sephardic coreligionists, they avoided non-kosher food, which in turn reduced potential conviviality with non-Jews (at least with those non-Jews who would have been willing to be friends with Jews). The men tended to wear beards, in accordance with the biblical prohibition against shaving. They therefore stood out in a society in which beards were unfashionable. Many also wore a distinctive style of dress that marked them as different or foreign.

Most Gentiles in Britain encountered Jews, if at all, only in business transactions.[4] For the wealthy who periodically needed cash to engage in such aristocratic pursuits as gambling, this might mean seeking out a Jewish (typically Sephardic) moneylender. (Barred for centuries from owning land and from most artisanal crafts, European Jews had taken recourse in the unpopular business of moneylending.) For the more modest non-Jewish Briton, an encounter with Jews might take place when shopping for goods at a Jewish-owned shop (such as the fruit shop in which Mendoza briefly worked), purchasing used apparel from an Ashkenazi "old clothes" man, or buying other items from a Jewish peddler.[5] Whether one borrowed or bought from Jews, accusations of unfair treatment were tempting. It was unsurprising that Gentiles complained that the interest rates on loans were too high or that the used products they bought were of lesser quality than promised.

---

[4]It should be noted that not all reluctance to socialize came from the Gentiles. Many Jews were suspicious of Gentiles and also worried that friendly contact might lead to intermarriage and the conversion of their children (especially daughters) to Christianity.

[5]Jewish peddlers were best known for selling used clothes, but they were also often described as selling oranges, lemons, rhubarb, pencils, paper, sealing wax, buttons, knives, razors, buckles, slippers, eyeglasses, jewelry, candy, and cakes. See Endelman, *Jews of Georgian England*, 180–81.

Old Clothes to fell; any Hats, Shoes, or Old Clothes?

An Ashkenazi "Old Clothes Man" depicted in an illustrated book about London trades, *The Cries of London* (London, 1796). (© The British Library Board, C. 194.a.30 pg. 16)

ANTI-SEMITISM AND TOLERANCE IN BRITISH SOCIETY

The word **anti-Semitism** is typically used to describe prejudice or discrimination against Jews. Though the word was only coined in the 1870s to indicate the racist belief that Jews belonged to a specific (and inferior) race of "Semites," in its conventional use it covers earlier, pre-racist bias against Jews. In this respect Britain, like other countries, exhibited a significant degree of anti-Semitism. William Shakespeare's famous play *The Merchant of Venice*, written between 1596 and 1598, featured the cruel Jewish moneylender Shylock who demanded a "pound of flesh" from a Christian debtor, and the popularity of the work seemed to encourage lesser writers and commentators to portray Jews in the same negative light.

In 1753 Parliament passed the Jewish Naturalization Bill (which King George II approved), thereby allowing foreign-born Jews to become British subjects without having to be baptized or to receive communion (the wafer believed to be the body of Christ) from the Church of England. But many Britons protested vehemently against the "Jew Bill." Numerous anti-Semitic pamphlets appeared repeating the accusations that Jews were greedy, dishonest and the eternal enemies of Christians. The bill's sponsors backed down in the face of this pressure and in 1754 Parliament repealed the law. Meanwhile, during the midst of the controversy ordinary Jews faced verbal abuse and the refusal of innkeepers to serve or lodge them.

Nor did anti-Semitism disappear in the years that followed. Festivities surrounding the king's birthday in 1763 degenerated into violence when a group of sailors and their supporters attacked the houses of Jews and assaulted their inhabitants in alleged retaliation for a pickpocketing by a Jew. In other incidents of the 1760s and 1770s Jews were forced to eat bacon (in violation of the Jewish prohibition on pork) or forcibly greased with pig fat.[6] The reformer and writer Francis Place remarked that "it was thought good sport to maltreat a Jew, and they were often most barbarously used [i.e., treated], even in the principal streets. . . . I have seen many [J]ews hooted, hunted, kicked, cuffed, pulled by the beard, spit up, and so barbarously assaulted in the streets, without any protection, from passers by, or the police."[7] And we have seen in Chapter 1 that Mendoza himself reported in his memoirs that the woman in whose fruit shop he briefly worked was "frequently" insulted "on account of . . . being of the Jewish religion." Under these circumstances it is reasonable to see Mendoza's acquisition of boxing skills as at least partially motivated by anti-Semitism.

---

[6]Endelman, *Jews of Georgian England*, 91, 115, 114.

[7]Jerry White, *London in the Eighteenth Century: A Great and Monstrous Thing* (London: Bodley Head, 2012), 151–52.

At the same time, there were clear limits to British anti-Semitism, and Jews in the eighteenth century enjoyed better treatment in Britain than in any other European country, with the possible exception of the Netherlands—though the economic growth of Britain and depression in the Netherlands gave Jews more opportunities in Britain. As the historian Todd Endelman observes, Jews "were not the objects of special laws, as they were elsewhere." It is true that they were not allowed to serve in Parliament or study at Oxford or Cambridge, but this was because they were not members of the Church of England, "not because they were Jews per se." Presbyterians, Quakers, Baptists, Methodists, and Catholics suffered from the same legal disabilities. Moreover, Endelman notes that even after the "Jew Bill" agitation Parliament did not pass any specifically anti-Jewish legislation, such as special taxes levied on the community, as was common in other countries and despite calls for such measures by anti-Semites.[8] This in itself is evidence of a strong tradition of religious tolerance.

Indeed, alongside anti-Semitism England had a tradition of **philo-Semitism**, or special concern for the plight of the Jews. Rooted in seventeenth-century English Protestantism, philo-Semitism held that England could hasten the Second Coming of Christ by gathering and welcoming the Jews. Like anti-Semitism, this term is an invention of later commentators and was not used in the eighteenth century. It can be confusing because philo-Semites saw the protection of the Jews as a step toward converting them to Christianity; thus they did not care for Jews *as Jews*. But this way of thinking, which may have influenced Cromwell to admit the Jews in the first place, also informed the writings of some pamphleteers at the time of the controversy over the Jewish Naturalization Bill. It arguably helped to prevent anti-Semitic action, as this might have led to an exodus of Jews from Britain and, in the thinking of philo-Semites, a failure to elicit the Second Coming.[9]

In addition, Endelman argues that a more secular force behind the relatively friendly atmosphere for Jews was the British embrace of commerce and its attendant philosophy of **liberalism**, which advocated personal freedoms, including freedom of religion, as necessary for the wealth and happiness of the people, and which saw religious bigotry as a hindrance to national prosperity. Here even the prejudice that labeled Jews as particularly suited to business served as an argument for treating them well in Britain.[10]

[8]Endelman, *Jews of Georgian England*, 45, 110.
[9]Endelman, *Jews of Georgian England*, 50–85.
[10]Endelman, *Jews of Georgian England*, 13–49.

Paradoxically, Mendoza's career may have been fueled by both anti-Semitism and tolerance. Anti-Semitism motivated Mendoza to learn to defend himself and his honor, as well as that of his coreligionists, while tolerance made it possible for him to earn the respect of his fellow British subjects for his excellence in boxing.

LEISURE, COMMERCE, AND THE RISE OF SPECTATOR SPORTS

Along with the context of Jewish history in Britain, the context of the history of sports is important in explaining Mendoza's career. Today we take sports for granted as a natural activity for many people to do and for even more to watch as spectators, but sports has a history, and eighteenth-century Britain was crucial to its development. In order for sports to develop, people have to have leisure—that is, the time to devote to an activity apart from work. Prior to the eighteenth century England was predominantly rural, and leisure activities therefore took place according to the rhythm of agriculture, with festivals occurring after planting season and at harvesting time. The Christian calendar also determined when people could take a rest from their labors and engage in leisure activities; thus villages held festivals at Shrovetide (known as Carnival in Catholic countries), Easter, and Whitsuntide (i.e., Pentecost). Various athletic contests, including races and ball games resembling modern soccer, were typically part of the festivities, but aspects we associate with modern sports were absent: there were no permanent teams, spectators did not pay for admission to events, no one made a living as an athlete (or promoter, for that matter), and any fame associated with sporting abilities was necessarily local and usually fleeting.

Leisure practices changed with the modernization of Britain in the eighteenth century. The rise of large-scale commercial agriculture pressured small farmers to seek their livelihood in towns and cities. Urban work had a different rhythm. Insofar as workers had leisure, it was limited to single days (often Mondays or Tuesdays) or even hours. Shopkeepers and professionals, even if they grew prosperous, had similar time pressures. The impulse to play, which the Dutch historian Johan Huizinga considered so essential to humanity that he coined the term *Homo Ludens* (roughly "man the player" or "man who plays"), was channeled into new activities.[11] City

---

[11] Johan Huizinga, *Homo Ludens: A Study of the Play Element in Culture* (Boston: Beacon Press, 1955).

dwellers could attend sports events such as cricket matches, horse races, or boxing matches, and it is not an accident that these three sports emerged in the eighteenth century.[12] And although most people *watched* rather than played these sports, they could obtain a sense of competing in the contests they observed by betting on them. Though the drive to wager money on a sporting outcome was no doubt driven by the desire to obtain more money, it also gave them a sense of being a part of the game. The emergence of new sports was part of what the historian J. H. Plumb called the "commercialisation of leisure."[13] Economic growth and urbanization in the eighteenth century meant that there was a market for leisure. When seeking leisure activities a city dweller might buy a ticket to the theater—and theaters emerged at an astonishing rate in the eighteenth century—or a ticket to a sporting event.

BOXING IN EIGHTEENTH-CENTURY BRITAIN

Advocates of boxing proudly traced the history of their sport to antiquity, noting that it existed in ancient Greece, as passages in Homer's epic poem *The Iliad* (eighth century BCE) suggest. But there is little evidence of the sport in England prior to the seventeenth century, when the diarist Samuel Pepys reported a match in 1660. By the 1720s boxing was becoming popular in London, where James Figg established an "academy," an amphitheater with the capacity to hold more than a thousand spectators. Figg excelled not only in boxing but also in other arts of "defence" including use of the back-sword (a wooden stick used in fencing) and cudgel (a wooden club), and in addition to performing himself employed others to display their skills before a paying audience. In 1743 Jack Broughton opened his own amphitheater, where he fought numerous challengers and mounted matches between other boxers. He charged a shilling, roughly half a day's wages for an average worker, thus excluding the working poor but providing affordable entertainment to middle-class and upper-class Londoners.

Broughton was an undefeated boxer for 24 years, but he is historically significant mainly because he wrote the first rules of boxing. Although in principle only applicable in his amphitheater, "Broughton's rules" became

---

[12]Dennis Brailsford, *A Taste for Diversions: Sport in Georgian England* (Cambridge, UK: Lutterworth Press, 1999).

[13]J[ohn] H[arold] Plumb, *The Commercialisation of Leisure in Eighteenth-Century England* (Reading, UK: Reading University, 1973); and Hugh Cunningham, *Leisure in the Industrial Revolution* (London: Croom Helm, 1980), 17.

something of a code of boxing for nearly a century. Broughton established the practice of drawing a square yard with chalk in the center of the "stage" and requiring the fighters to approach the yard within 30 seconds after falling. (Rounds ended only after a boxer fell, not after a uniform period of time.) In addition, he stipulated "that no person is to hit his adversary when he is down, or seize him by the ham, the breeches, or any part below

Jack Broughton (c. 1703–89) was a champion pugilist and promoter of his sport. (©National Portrait Gallery, London)

the waist; a man on his knees to be reckoned down."[14] Still, Broughton's rules were relatively sparse, and much that is forbidden in modern boxing was allowed. Broughton did not prohibit wrestling moves or clinching. He was silent on kicking, scratching, biting, and gouging, all of which would be explicitly forbidden in the mid-nineteenth century. Dangerous blows that are prohibited today, such as "rabbit punches" (just below the ear) and kidney punches, were allowed. (In fact, in his book on boxing Mendoza even recommended kidney punches!)[15] Moreover, there were no rules concerning boxing gloves, as they were worn only for sparring and not during matches.

Boxing went into decline in the 1750s, for reasons that historians are not entirely clear on. (According to the early nineteenth-century sports journalist and historian Pierce Egan, the Duke of Cumberland lost thousands of pounds on a match at Broughton's amphitheater and retaliated by having it closed, though more recently the sports historian Tony Gee has noted that the institution remained in existence for the next three years.[16]) Broughton's academy was closed in 1754, though it is unclear whether the closure was for legal or financial reasons. In any event, thereafter the authorities typically treated boxing as an illegal activity. Although no law specifically prohibited boxing, judicial magistrates could interpret any match as a duel, an "affray" (assault), a disturbance of the peace or a riot, all of which were decidedly illegal. And increasingly this is how the authorities treated the sport. By the mid-1770s all boxing exhibitions in permanent or semipermanent locations (such as amphitheaters and circus grounds) had been closed, and the future of the sport looked unpromising.[17]

But boxing made a dramatic comeback in the late 1780s. Judicial authorities continued to treat the sport as illegal. (We have seen in Chapter 3 of the graphic history how a magistrate intervened to stop a contest between Mendoza and Humphries in Epping Forest.) It is for this reason that the location of a match was kept secret until shortly before the fight and that matches were typically fought far away from London and other cities. What accounts for the sport's resurgence despite its marginal legal status? The taste of powerful backers was particularly important. Indeed, one of

---

[14]Pierce Egan, *Boxiana; Or, Sketches of Ancient and Modern Pugilism* (London, 1830), vol. 1, pp. 51–52.

[15]Daniel Mendoza, *The Art of Boxing: With a Statement of the Transactions that Have Passed between Mr. Humphreys and Myself Since our Battle at Odiham* (London, 1789), 23.

[16]Tony Gee, "Broughton, John," *Oxford Dictionary of National Biography* (online): http://www.oxforddnb.com/view/article/3586

[17]Brailsford, *Taste for Diversions*, 33.

boxing's greatest fans was none other than the Prince of Wales, who as the eldest son of King George III would later reign as George IV (1820–30).[18] The king's two other sons—the Duke of York and the future King William IV (reigned 1830–37)— were also boxing enthusiasts and patrons.[19] They wielded influence over the sport in two ways. The first was simply monetary: by providing the prize money for matches and raising money from their rich, aristocratic friends, they made it possible for high-stakes matches such as the one depicted in Chapter 1 between Mendoza and Martin the Butcher. Second, then—as now—the royal family (along with other upper-class people) played a large role in determining what was fashionable. For those who felt a need to be seen among the elite in British society, the presence of royals at a boxing match must have been highly motivating. Further down the hierarchy patrons included earls, lords, and gentlemen with the title of "Sir," as well as colonels and captains. This is not to say that social influence was strictly from the top down. Patrons seem to have had real admiration for the professional boxers, who stemmed almost exclusively from the lowest rungs of society, and whose sport clearly had modest origins, though their snobbery sometimes got the best of them (as when Mendoza showed his modest origins by making mistakes during a fox hunt—depicted in Chapter 3) and their willingness to mix was certainly limited.

If the patrons of the sport were notably upper class and the boxers them-selves of modest origins, the spectators came from a broad mix of classes. Of course, the poorest people in British society needed to work every hour possible, and the time needed to attend a match at a remote location would have been prohibitive, to say nothing of the cost of transportation, food, and (depending on the distance traveled) lodging. Moreover, the entrance tickets for the most anticipated fights cost half a guinea each, or about a week's wages for an artisan. Still, the prospect of winning a bet on a match no doubt lured some men (and contemporary accounts suggest that audi-ences were overwhelmingly male) to think that they might break even or even make a profit by going to the match, and we know from reports on the Mendoza-Humphries match at Doncaster (depicted in Chapter 5) that many fans did not buy tickets and simply broke through the gates.

---

[18]The Prince of Wales also served as Prince Regent during his father's mental illness (1811–20). Thus he reigned for two decades.

[19]Brailsford writes of "the three sons of George III" that "the rapid revival of the [sic] pugilism in the later 1780s undoubtedly owed very much to their support." *Taste for Diversions*, 95.

THE ROLE OF NATIONALISM

Another factor in the popularization of boxing, and hence in Mendoza's career, was **nationalism**. Today it seems "natural" that people belong to nations, that they form identities based largely on this sense of belonging, and that loyalty to a nation is considered a virtue. But these ideas were new in the eighteenth century. Prior to that time most people were more likely to identify with their town or village, or with their craft or profession, or with their family, clan, or social caste, than they were with any "nation." Many subjects felt or displayed loyalty to the monarch, or in some cases to the idea of a "state," but this was different from identifying with the people within the boundaries of that state.

This began to change in the eighteenth century. Among the first to proclaim national allegiances were French and British subjects. They did so against the backdrop of a series of wars between France and Britain. During the course of these conflicts, French and British nationalists formed their identities largely in terms of what they were *not*. Thus during the Seven Years' War (1756–63), as David Bell has shown, French writers defined themselves as *not* treacherous "barbarians" like their British enemies.[20] Likewise, British subjects, so often elicited in the century's conflicts with the French, came to think of themselves as a distinct nation. If the French were slaves to an absolute monarch, the British were free—their king was limited in his power by a Parliament. Moreover, as Linda Colley has shown, eighteenth-century Britons made much of their Protestant faith, contrasting it with the supposedly "fanatical" and "superstitious" Catholic Church that held sway in France.[21]

What does all this have to do with boxing? Advocates of the sport promoted it by labeling it "British." They claimed that it was characteristic of the British in particular to settle their disputes with their fists. In this they implicitly or explicitly contrasted the British sport of boxing with the supposedly French habit of dueling with swords or pistols. In the first history of pugilism, written in 1812, Pierce Egan included it among "those sports that tend to invigorate the human frame, and inculcate those principles of generosity and heroism, by which the inhabitants of the English Nation

---

[20]"The war literature of the 1750s and 1760s, for the first time in French history, presented an international conflict neither as a duel between royal houses nor as a clash of religions, but as a battle between irreconcilable nations." David A. Bell, *The Cult of the Nation in France: Inventing Nationalism, 1680–1800* (Cambridge, MA: Harvard University Press, 2001), 80.

[21]Linda Colley, *Britons: Forging the Nation, 1707–1837* (New Haven, CT: Yale University Press, 1992), esp. 11–54.

are so eminently distinguished above every other country."[22] While this comment referred to England rather than Britain, and thereby seemed to exclude Scotland and Wales from consideration, elsewhere Egan frequently praised his fellow *Britons*. Thus to those who listened to criticisms of the sport as brutal or uncivilized he urged, "Never let Britons be ashamed of . . . a science that not only adds generosity to their disposition—humanity to their conduct—but courage to their national character. A country where the stiletto is not known—where trifling quarrels do not produce assassination, and where revenge is not finished by murder."[23] The reference to the stiletto was an implicit criticism of Italians, but Egan also railed against the French for dueling. He was outraged that the Vicomte de Mirabeau (1754–92), a nobleman and brother of a famous revolutionary lawmaker, was able to insult people with impunity and even seduce their wives and daughters simply because he had become skilled at dueling. Such a situation would have been impossible in Britain, according to Egan, since men would have had the chance to defend their honor and that of their female relatives by engaging in boxing contests with the seducer.[24]

Mendoza himself praised boxing as a British sport. In his book *The Art of Boxing* (1789), he lauded it as "a national mode of combat," one that was "as peculiar to the inhabitants of this country as *Fencing* to the French."[25] In the preface to his memoirs he wrote proudly that "this country is the only one in which pugilism has been wrought into a regular system, and elevated to the rank of a science," and added, in a plea to the authorities to stop suppressing the sport, "That the art of pugilism is peculiar to this country, will not be disputed. In other countries, contests of a more dangerous, but of a less hardy and vigorous kind, are suffered and patronized; why then should we be prevented from exercising an art, well adapted to promote health—to give courage to the timid—to repress insolence[,] and to enable men to stand in their own defence against the assaults they are daily exposed to?"[26]

---

[22]Egan, *Boxiana*, vol. 1, pp. iii–iv.

[23]Egan, *Boxiana*, vol. 1, p. 2. Comments such as this one confirm Linda Colley's claim that a specifically *British* national identity emerged in the eighteenth and early nineteenth centuries. See her *Britons*, passim.

[24]Egan, *Boxiana*, vol. 1, pp. 10–11.

[25]*The Art of Boxing: With a Statement of the Transactions that Have Passed between Mr. Humphreys and Myself Since our Battle at Odiham* (London, 1789), vi–vii.

[26]Daniel Mendoza, *Memoirs of the Life of Daniel Mendoza; Containing a Faithful Narrative of the Various Vicissitudes of his Life, and an Account of the Numerous Contests in which he has been Engaged, with Observations on Each; Comprising also Genuine Anecdotes of Many Distinguished Characters, to which are Added, Observations on the Art of Pugilism; Rules to be Observed with Regard to Training, &c* (London, 1816), xvi.

Mendoza's nationalism is not surprising. As we have seen, despite the problem of anti-Semitism, Britain was more welcoming to the Jews than most if not all other European countries. It was certainly a marked contrast to the land of his ancestors, where the practice of Judaism was illegal and where the Inquisition was still in operation (until 1834). This is not to say that Mendoza became a boxer *because* he was a British nationalist, but that his chosen profession fit comfortably with his feelings for Britain.

THE ROLE OF GENDER

A final context is necessary for an understanding of Mendoza's life and career: gender. Historian Joan Scott defines gender both as "a constitutive element of social relationships based on perceived differences between the sexes" and "a primary way of signifying relationships of power."[27] This means that how people relate to one another in society is determined by what they understand to be "masculine" or "feminine" characteristics. Moreover, these definitions will have an important say in how much power certain people or groups have. Mendoza and other supporters of boxing characterized the sport as "manly," and students of history should pay close attention to this term. This doesn't mean we should ask whether it was *truly* manly; rather, we should ask how this description functioned. For the advocates of boxing, as for others in eighteenth-century British society, to call something "manly" was to praise and legitimize it. This asserted not only the power of men over women, but the power of groups participating in supposedly "manly" activities over those whose traits or practices were thought to be "effeminate."

The implications of gender for power relations can be even more clearly seen when analyzing its connection to nationalism. When praising their "nation" and making claims about what it was or should be, Britons used gendered language. And advocates of boxing attempted to legitimize their sport by linking it to the "manly" British nation. Thus in 1743 John Broughton, the early boxing champion and rule maker discussed above, wrote a pamphlet significantly titled, *Proposals for Erecting an Amphitheatre for the Manly Exercise of Boxing.* In it he wrote, "BRITONS then who boast themselves Inheritors of the *Greek* and *Roman* Virtues, should follow their Example, and by encouraging Conflicts of this magnanimous

---

[27]Joan Scott, "Gender: A Useful Category of Historical Analysis," *American Historical Review* 91 (December 1986): 1067.

Kind [i.e., boxing matches], endeavour to eradicate that *foreign Effeminacy* which has so fatally insinuated itself among us, and almost destroy'd that glorious Spirit of *British Championism*, which was wont to be at once the *Terror* and *Disgrace* of our Enemies."[28] Here we see gendered language at work. The legitimate, praiseworthy group is described as British and manly; all others are dismissed as foreign and effeminate.

Egan similarly paired manliness and nationality when he wrote that "the manly art of Boxing has infused that true heroic courage, blended with humanity, into the hearts of Britons, which have made them so renowned, terrific, and triumphant, in all parts of the world." Elsewhere he wrote, "We have long witnessed the good effects of this manly spirit in England, and we trust it will never be extinguished."[29] There are many other references to manliness in Egan's history of boxing. In fact the word "manly" occurs 68 times and "manliness" occurs 17 times in the first volume only!

Mendoza himself referred to boxing as "this manly art," and when he complained about Humphries's uninvited visit to his academy shortly after the death of Mendoza's daughter (depicted in Chapter 4 of the graphic history), he asked rhetorically whether such behavior was "manly."[30] His attachment to the language of manliness is understandable. Challenges to fight were perceived as challenges to a contestant's masculinity. Moreover, insofar as manliness was connected to membership in the nation and foreigners were seen as "effeminate," men whose nationality was questioned doubtless felt pressure to assert both their attachment to the nation and their masculinity. We have already seen that not all British people accepted the Jews as members of their nation, and as a Jew with a Hispanic name Mendoza could be seen as doubly foreign. Embracing a sport that was both "national" and "manly" may have been a way for him to feel part of a powerful group.

---

[28]John Broughton, *Proposals for Erecting an Amphitheatre for the Manly Exercise of Boxing, by John Broughton, Professor of Athletics* [London], [1743], 1. Emphasis in the original.

[29]Egan, *Boxiana*, vol. 1, pp. 3, 13.

[30]Mendoza, *Memoirs*, xvi; and *Art of Boxing*, 67.

PART IV

THE MAKING OF
MENDOZA THE JEW

א

One of the goals of the book *Mendoza the Jew* is to give you an understanding of how the discipline of history works. What do historians do, and how do they do it? You have already learned about the importance of primary sources in the creation of reliable accounts of the past, and in Part II you have read some of these sources. In Part V you will have the chance to use them and thereby do the kind of work that professional historians do—in other words, you will be creating secondary sources. But before we get there I (Ronald) would like to provide you with more of a sense of how a work of history is produced. I cannot speak for all historians, and I am not comfortable issuing rules and regulations, but I can tell you the story of how I became interested in Mendoza, how I went about my research, and how Liz and I produced the book you are now reading.

In the fall of 2005 my university library acquired a database called Eighteenth Century Collections Online (ECCO), a massive digital library of roughly 200,000 volumes that were published in Britain and its colonies between the years 1701 and 1800. ECCO is word-searchable, so it is possible to find references to hundreds or even thousands of books containing any given term. You can enter a word like "liberty" or "revolution" or "horse" or "coffee" or "widow" and immediately find yourself reading a primary source in which the term was used. For me the process was addictive, and I spent many idle hours immersing myself in the eighteenth century in this way. I can't remember what term I entered when ECCO led me to *The Art of Boxing* (1789), by Daniel Mendoza, but I remember being fascinated by the book. I knew very little about the history of sports, and I was surprised to see that boxing was such a popular sport in the eighteenth century. (The fact that several editions of Mendoza's book appeared within a few years attests to the popularity of the sport.) I noted with interest that the author classified the sport as *British* and contrasted it with French fencing. I wondered what sort of person might have read *The Art of Boxing,* and why. And I was curious to learn more about the author.

ECCO AND THE LURE OF PRIMARY SOURCES

So I entered the term "Mendoza" in the search engine and began reading in hundreds of books that referred to the boxer. One of them was a novel in which a character speculated that an aggressive man "had been taking a lesson from Mendoza."[1] I knew from the *Art of Boxing* that Mendoza gave boxing lessons; this novel suggested that both the boxer and his school were sufficiently well known for an author to expect readers to recognize the references. The database also led me to a poem called "The Muses in Motion," in which the Muse of Tragedy and that of Comedy competed for their theater audience's affection. The Muse of Comedy addressed the spectators:

> Since then you cannot take us both in keeping,
> Which Miss shall stay, the laughing, or the weeping?
> If me ye choose, kind Sirs, for *cara Sposa* [dear wife],
> I'll instant tip my Sister a *Mendoza*.[2]

The stage direction here required the Comic Muse to hold up her fists. Between this source and others I came to learn that to tip someone a Mendoza meant to punch him or her.[3] A third source I found in ECCO was a poem written in Oxford that included these lines:

> You must know that Mendoza has been in this town,
> To manage the fists of the lads of the gown.[4]

I learned only later that Mendoza had in fact visited Oxford in November 1789, to great acclaim, and won a match against a cabinetmaker who was two to three stones (28 to 42 pounds) heavier.[5] The evidence was mounting that readers as well as theater audiences knew Mendoza well. I wanted to know him just as well.

---

[1] *Adeline; or the Orphan* (London, 1790), vol. 1, p. 200.

[2] Miles Peter Andrews, "The Muses in Motion, Spoken at the Royalty Theatre, by Mrs. Hudson and Mrs. Gibbs. In the Characters of the Tragic and Comic Muse," in *The European Magazine, and London Review; Containing the Literature, History, Politics, Arts, Manners and Amusements of the Age....* (London, 1788), vol. 13, p. 57.

[3] According to one newspaper children threatened each other by saying, "I'll tip you Mendoza." *Diary or Woodfall's Register,* Tuesday, September 8, 1789, Issue 140.

[4] "Epistle from Quondam in the Country, to his Cousin Quoz. By an Oxford Correspondent," *The Attic Miscellany; and Characteristic Mirror of Men and Things. Including the Correspondent's Museum. Volume the First* (London, 1791), 153. The expression "lads of the gown" refers to the Oxford University students, who wore specific gowns indicating their status as students.

[5] *English Chronicle or Universal Evening Post*, November 24–26, 1789.

Something else piqued my curiosity in the poem about the Oxford visit. The poet referred to Mendoza (more than once) as "the Jew." Other sources, including Mendoza's memoirs, confirmed that the boxer was indeed Jewish. This raised a new set of questions. What did Mendoza's Jewishness mean to boxing spectators and the British reading public? What did it mean to Mendoza? How was it possible for a Jew with a Hispanic name to become a hero in a British national sport? What did this say about British culture at the time? Mendoza's Jewishness was particularly interesting to me because I had long been interested in Jewish history. I had written a book about the Jews of France.[6] Perhaps I could write something, at least an article, on a Jewish boxer from Britain.

THE SEARCH FOR SECONDARY SOURCES

But before I could write anything about Mendoza I needed to know what other historians had written about him. In other words, I needed to move from primary to secondary sources. The first stop in any search for secondary sources is FirstSearch, a bibliographic database maintained by OCLC (Online Computer Library Center) that contains over 250 million catalogue records from libraries around the world. Any books about Mendoza would be sure to appear in this database. But when I entered "Mendoza, Daniel" as a subject I found only two books: a brief biography written for a children's audience in 1962 and Mendoza's own memoirs (in other words, another primary source).[7]

So I looked for another kind of secondary source: articles. The best place to begin looking for articles is JSTOR, a digital library that includes all the issues (with the exception of the most recent few years) of over 1400 scholarly journals; it contains more than 8 million articles. But when I searched the database I found only one article specifically on Mendoza. Titled simply "Daniel Mendoza," it was the published version of a lecture delivered by Lewis Edwards to the Jewish Historical Society of England on March 15, 1938.[8]

I learned a lot from Edwards's article. The author had done considerable research on Mendoza's family, from his *shochet* (ritual slaughterer)

---

[6]Ronald Schechter, *Obstinate Hebrews: Representations of Jews in France, 1715–1815* (Berkeley: University of California Press, 2003).

[7]Harold U. Ribalow, *Fighter from Whitechapel: The Story of Daniel Mendoza* (New York: Farrar, Straus and Cudahy, 1962). Illustrated by Simon Jeruchim.

[8]Lewis Edwards, "Daniel Mendoza," in *The Jewish Historical Society of England. Transactions: Sessions 1939–1945* (London: Edward Goldston, 1946), vol. 15, pp. 73–92.

grandfather to his parents, wife, and children. In addition to reading Mendoza's memoirs, Edwards had consulted the circumcision and marriage records of the Spanish and Portuguese Synagogue (also called the Bevis Marks Synagogue), and from these he painstakingly constructed the boxer's genealogy.[9] Yet when it came to the Mendoza's historical significance, Edwards had little to say. He merely concluded that "one who in a profession and in circumstances where lapses from the straight path of virtue were common did on the whole bear himself worthily and well, and above all demonstrated to a not too friendly world, not always prompt to believe it, that Judaism and courage often go together."[10] This conclusion struck me as uninteresting. In order for an argument to be interesting, there have to be people seriously claiming the contrary. But no one would seriously claim that Judaism and courage are incompatible. No one but anti-Semites, and it might be best not to dignify their claims with arguments to the contrary.[11]

ABINA, NEWSPAPER DATABASES, AND OXFORD UNIVERSITY PRESS

But it's easy to criticize another historian. Could I do better? I wasn't sure. I felt that it might be possible to use the Mendoza story as a window onto larger issues in eighteenth-century history such as nationalism and gender, but I wasn't sure I had enough to say about the subject to justify an extended study. I had a rich trove of sources in the ECCO database, but I didn't know whether this would suffice. Meanwhile other commitments competed for my attention, including several projects in French history, and I set Mendoza aside.

Then roughly five years later I came back to Mendoza and began working in earnest on the book you are now reading. Why? In the fall of 2011 I was teaching a global history course when Karlyn Hixson, a representative from Oxford University Press, gave me a copy of a book called *Abina and the Important Men*. This "graphic history," written by Trevor Getz and

---

[9]These records were subsequently translated from the Hebrew and published. Lionel D. Barnett et al., *Bevis Marks Records: Being Contributions to the History of the Spanish and Portuguese Congregation of London* (Oxford: Oxford University Press, 1940), 6 vols.

[10]Edwards, "Mendoza," 92.

[11]In fairness to Edwards, he was researching this topic at a time when Hitler had begun his massive persecution of Jews in Germany. In fact, his lecture took place on the very day (March 15) that Hitler annexed Austria. And there were anti-Semitic parties endangering Jews in many other countries, including Britain. So it is understandable that Edwards, and no doubt his audience, wanted to celebrate the courage of a Jew who had lived in his country in the past.

illustrated by Liz Clarke is about a young woman named Abina from the Gold Coast (today Ghana) who took her employer to court for illegally enslaving her. The book immediately drew me in. The artwork was stunning, and the book was accompanied by the primary source (the court record) on which the story was based, as well as essays on historical context and historical method. I saw in the book not only an opportunity to teach aspects of global history (especially imperialism and slavery), but also a chance to introduce students to the craft of history more broadly. I assigned the book to my class in the spring of 2012, and students responded to it very favorably. I was so taken by the form of the book that I began to think about what might be the subject of another "graphic history" and whether I might be able to write the text for it.

I immediately thought of Mendoza. I could picture him (in the style of Liz's drawings) on the page, punching Richard Humphries and blocking blows from him, courting Esther, riding "among the hounds" with his would-be aristocratic friends, trying his hand at various trades and businesses, and finding himself before judges and in jail. Moreover, a new development in what is now called "digital humanities" made the project appear more feasible to me. Specifically, two new massive databases of British newspapers made it possible to read hundreds of contemporary press reports about Mendoza. One of the databases, called 17th and 18th Century Burney Collection Newspapers, is based on the collection of the Reverend Charles Burney (1757–1817) at the British Library. It contains over a million pages and is word searchable. The second database, 19th Century British Library Newspapers, contains over 2 million pages and is similarly word-searchable. I was extremely fortunate that my university library purchased access to both databases. Indeed, the work I have done for this book would not have been possible without access to them. I would not have known nearly as many details about Mendoza's life and career. Also, most of the primary sources in Part II come from the newspapers in the Burney Collection database.

THE AUTHOR AND THE ILLUSTRATOR BEGIN THEIR COLLABORATION: THE FIRST PAGE OF *MENDOZA THE JEW*

So I approached Karlyn, and she put me in touch with Charles Cavaliere, the acquisitions editor for world history textbooks. I pitched my idea to him, and he encouraged me to put together a proposal with Liz. He introduced me (electronically) to Liz, and we began work on the proposal, which included (among other things) a sample chapter of the graphic history along with the entire text of the graphic history and descriptions of the images Liz would create.

Before I could present any ideas to Liz I had to conduct additional research. I reread sources such as Mendoza's memoirs and his *Art of Boxing.* I consulted books in the ECCO database as well, and I did a thorough search of the articles on Mendoza in the two newspaper databases mentioned above. I had the good fortune to have a skilled and diligent research assistant, Sagra Alvarado, and together we transcribed hundreds of articles featuring Mendoza. From these sources I began to write a narrative of Mendoza's life. At first I wrote as though I were constructing a traditional, strictly textual (as opposed to graphic) biography, with details that solidified my understanding of the events, personalities, challenges, and other phenomena that made up Mendoza's life. As I set out to recount Mendoza's biography I simply wrote what I knew from the sources, proceeding in chronological order, without worrying about which events would make it into the graphic history.

Finally I was ready to present my ideas to Liz. This process consisted of several tasks. For each frame, or "cell," I described the image, sometimes roughly and sometimes in more detail, that I was looking for. Then I added text, either in the form of a narrative box or a speech bubble. In addition, I provided as much visual material as possible so that Liz's renditions would be historically accurate. We didn't want eighteenth-century people to be wearing nineteenth-century clothes, for example.

One way to show how this collaboration worked is to recall the process of producing the first page of the graphic history. In my mind's eye I saw the first frame: a boxing ring at Barnet Common, with Mendoza and Martin the Butcher, along with their seconds and bottle-holders and the umpires, on the stage. How could I convey this image to Liz? I began by writing (in a document attached to an email):

Cell 1.

Image: A boxing ring at Barnet Common, April 17, 1787. A match between Daniel "the Jew" Mendoza and Martin "the Bath Butcher." Barnet Common was the "common" land, or green space, in the town of Barnet, 10 miles north of central London.

From contemporary documents I had learned that the ring would have been 24 feet square and that it would have had rails, not ropes. I conveyed this information to Liz and added an image of the Gillray print (see Document 1.14 in Part II) depicting the first match between Mendoza and Humphries. Since no contemporary image of the Mendoza-Martin match existed, at least not to my knowledge, the Gillray print would have to suffice. These were my comments to Liz:

> Here's an image of a boxing stage. It's from a different fight . . . and it contains some elements of caricature, but I'm including it so you can see what the stage and rails looked like. This should also give you a sense of how the boxers dressed. The spectators will probably be indistinct in the first image, but they would have been mostly (not exclusively) men, including wealthy "gentlemen" but also working class Jews and (non-Jewish) butchers. . . .

> Also note how crowded the stage is: each fighter has a "second" and a "bottle-holder" to help him if necessary. There are also three umpires: one chosen by each fighter and a third chosen by the umpires themselves. So there will be nine men on the stage at any one time. (The above picture only has eight.) Other things you will no doubt notice: the fighters are bare-chested and wear knee-breeches with silk stockings and ordinary shoes with buckles. . . . Humphries has ribbons on his shoes, something newspaper reports also noticed. The seconds and bottle-holders are fully dressed, and the umpires have coats, hats and boots. Crucially, the boxers do not wear gloves. They are "bare-knuckle" boxers.

Finally, I added the text to appear in the narrative box: "Barnet Common, a field north of London. April 17, 1787."

For the second frame I simply wanted a picture of Mendoza holding up his fists in a defensive position. In order to give Liz a sense of what Mendoza looked like, I sent her several contemporary images of him, including one by Gillray, now in the Jewish Museum in London (see following page).

But since pictures of Mendoza tended to be idealized or caricatured, I noted, "Mendoza probably would have had puffy eyes (as boxer's tried to blind their opponents with blows to the eyes) and cuts on his face. His fists might also have been red (from his own blood and that of Martin)." As you can see from the first page of the graphic history, Liz did a splendid job of swelling and bloodying Mendoza in this manner. I also noted, drawing on contemporary newspaper reports, that Mendoza was 5 feet 7 inches and 146 pounds. (He would later gain weight.) Finally I added the text for the narrative box: "Daniel Mendoza was from a Jewish neighborhood in working-class East London. Known simply as 'Mendoza the Jew,' he was one of Britain's most promising boxers."

James Gillray's depiction of Mendoza (© Jewish Museum London).

The third frame proved more challenging, as I could not find any contemporary images of Martin the Butcher. So I wrote the following:

Cell 3.

Image: Martin "the Bath Butcher" throwing a punch with his right fist. (We're facing him, as if we were Mendoza.)

Unfortunately we don't know what Martin looked like. He was a butcher by trade and therefore accustomed to lifting heavy pork or mutton carcasses and cutting through bones. . . . From descriptions we know he was a little shorter than average, but so was Mendoza, so the men should be roughly the same height. But I would expect Martin to have been at least 20 pounds heavier. He was, after all, a two-to-one favorite in the fight. As far as facial features were concerned, this is up to your imagination. A boxer had typically broken his nose, in some cases multiple times, and once the fight had started he would have accumulated numerous cuts and bruises. His eyelids also would have been swollen, as boxers usually tried to blind their opponents. And of course it would be dramatic if he had a menacing look on his face.

Text (narrative box):

Sam Martin was a butcher from the city of Bath, England and as a boxer was ranked number two in Britain. In this match bets were in his favor by a two-to-one margin.

The rest of the page was relatively easy (for me, at least). I had given Liz as much information as I could about the setting and the boxers. Now I could let her describe some action:

Cell 4.

Image: Mendoza blocks the punch with his left forearm.

Text (narrative box):

Martin was strong and threw frequent punches, but Mendoza was quicker and more agile. He could avoid or block punches, and then, when his opponent was off-balance . . .

Cell 5.

Image: Mendoza punches Martin in the stomach, knocking the wind out of him.

Text (narrative box):

He delivered a swift, powerful blow to the gut, often following up . . .

Cell 6.

Image: Mendoza has just punched Martin in the face. Martin is falling onto the stage.

Text (narrative box):

with a punishing punch to the face.

Liz responded with the sketch on the following page.

I was thrilled, and even more so when Liz converted her sketch into inked artwork. It was as if she had read my mind. Even better, it was as if she had perceived the vague outlines of my imagination, clarified the pictures and improved on them with her own artistic skill and vision. I was excited to continue our collaboration. Only 9 more pages to go before we could submit the first chapter with the book proposal. I outlined each frame and sent Liz an abundance of visual material: prints of boxing matches, portraits of figures who appeared in the story (such as the Prince of Wales, the Marquess of Buckingham, Menasseh Ben Israel, Oliver Cromwell, and Richard Humphries), images of London architecture, maps, and pictures relating to the history of the Jews, prints featuring Jewish religious ceremonies and paraphernalia, prints depicting crafts (such as the many jobs Mendoza briefly worked at), images of period clothing,[12] and photographs of furniture, guinea coins, antique tobacco jars, and tea crates. All this material and my accompanying commentary resulted in a file that was 36 pages long and approximately 5000 words, though the text in first chapter of the graphic history came to roughly 2000 words. Liz supplemented these images with many additional ones that she found while doing her own research.

THE COLLABORATION CONTINUES

Yet it would be wrong to imagine that I simply fed Liz images and she converted them into drawings. She added numerous details, such as: the umpire's watch on page 2, panel 1; the cautious crypto-Jew peering through the shutters while his family celebrates a Jewish festival or Sabbath dinner on page 4, panel 3; and the smoke coming from the chimneys on page 10. She also interpreted the story through the characters' facial expressions and gestures, created moods with her choice of color (as in the

---

[12]Many of these images came from the Berg Fashion Archive, a database to which my university library subscribes.

MENDOZA THE JEW--PAGE #1--LIZ CLARKE 2012

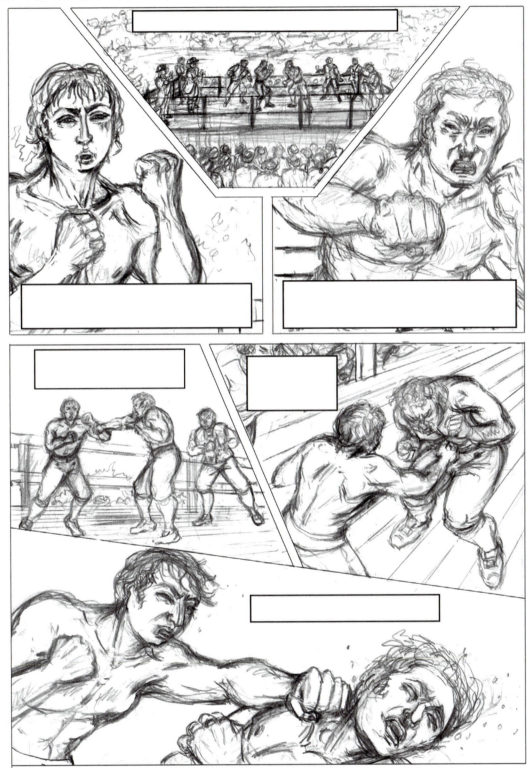

hot yellow-orange of the glassmaking workshop on page 6, panel 2, where things and people get literally and figuratively heated), and varied the size and shape of the panels in a way that creates a sense of movement and action. In other words, she took advantage of all the elements of the graphic form and produced something that went far beyond my promptings.

Liz also asked questions that resulted in an improved product. For example, when I described my idea for the picture of Mendoza at his Bar Mitzvah, I sent Liz pictures of a Torah scroll, a pointer (for reading the Torah), and a prayer shawl, or *tallit*. She asked, "For Daniel's Bar Mitzvah, would his prayer shawl be worn over his shoulders only, while the adult men in the synagogue wear theirs over their heads? Would Daniel have a skullcap while they wear their normal hats? Would we see tefillin being worn at all?" These questions prompted me to do more research into the prayer customs of eighteenth-century Sephardic Jews. The matter of the prayer shawl was easily solved when I looked at contemporary images of Sephardic worship: the shawls would indeed have been worn over the head, not simply around the shoulder. Regarding skullcaps, I learned that they came into usage among European Jews only in the nineteenth century, and that for eighteenth-century Jews the requirement that men cover their heads while praying was met by simply wearing the hats they would wear outdoors. In this way Liz's question saved us from the anachronistic picture of an eighteenth-century Jew in nineteenth-century attire. As to tefillin, I hadn't thought about that at all. Tefillin, otherwise known as phylacteries, consist of two black leather boxes containing Biblical verses. Adult Jewish men (including the one celebrating his Bar Mitzvah) wear one of the boxes on their head and the other on their left arm. A depiction of a synagogue service without tefillin would have been inaccurate, and Liz prevented this error by asking questions about its placement.

Once the first chapter of the graphic history was completed, I wrote the text for the remaining six chapters and provided descriptions of each of the cells, using a spreadsheet to create a kind of textual storyboard (see table on the following page).

THE SHAPING OF THE STORY AND CRITICAL READING OF THE SOURCES

While outlining the graphic history I had to be selective about which events to include for creating an engaging narrative. I determined that the dramatic action should be centered on the conflict between Mendoza and Humphries; after all, contemporaries tended to think of Humphries when they thought of Mendoza. Furthermore, just as screenplays are traditionally

CHAPTER 2: BOXING LESSONS (GRAPHIC SHEETS 11–19)

GRAPHIC SHEET NUMBER	CELL	IMAGE	TEXT	TEXT TYPE
11	1	Mendoza's boxing "academy" at 4, Capel Court in East London. A long line has formed outside.	Out of respect for the wishes of his fiancée Esther, Mendoza tried to reduce the number of prize fights he participated in. He invested his money in a business that he hoped would bring in a steady income: a boxing "academy."	Narrative box
	2	A teenage boy speaking.	I can't wait to see Mendoza's demonstration. Once we learn how to box, we won't have to worry about people insulting us for being Jewish anymore.	Speech bubble
	3	A second teenage boy	That's right. My father gave me a shilling to pay for my admission ticket. He said I didn't have to pay it back if I learned something useful.	Speech bubble
	4	The first teenage boy	What's more useful than self-defense, especially in this neighborhood? I'm saving up to pay for a private lesson. Half a guinea is a lot of money, but I think it'll be worth it. By the way, why doesn't your father come to Mendoza's academy himself?	Speech bubble
	5	The second teenage boy	He's pious. He spends Saturdays in the synagogue. He's not happy about this demonstration being on the Sabbath. But he couldn't have thought it was that bad, if he gave me a shilling to attend!	Speech bubble
	6	The first teenage boy	My mother also gave me a look when I told her I was going to see Mendoza on a Saturday. But this is the only day we have a break from work! Besides, the Good Lord can't think it's bad for his Chosen People to learn how to protect themselves and the honor of their religion! That has to be more important than the day of the week we learn these skills. Oh, look, they're opening the doors!	Speech bubble

divided into three acts, the history of this rivalry conveniently seemed to come in three "acts," one for each of the matches: at Odiham, Stilton, and Doncaster. It seemed natural to me to place one chapter for each of these contests at the center of the story—in other words, in chapters 3, 4, and

5. For chapters 1 and 2 I focused on events that provided background for understanding the protagonist, and for chapters 6 and 7 I selected events that seemed to conclude the story and establish its historical significance. Meanwhile, throughout the narrative I selected material describing the subplot of the relationship between Daniel and Esther.

When envisioning the images and producing the text I tried to stay as close to the sources as possible. There is documentary evidence to support the principal events of the story. Mendoza really did defeat Martin the Butcher at Barnet Common and win approximately a thousand pounds. The Prince of Wales and the Marquess of Buckingham were actually present at the match. His supporters really did celebrate his return to London by carrying him on their shoulders and singing triumphant songs. He engaged in all the jobs described in the graphic history. All of the boxing matches described in the book really took place. The members of his family mentioned in the book really existed, and Mendoza did appear before judges and spend time in jail.

If at all possible I tried to corroborate claims—in other words, find more than one source that said the same thing, especially if the claim seemed unlikely to me. For example, the *World* newspaper reported that following the match at Stilton "HUMPHRIES has lately had a *paralytic stroke;* and from which he has not, nor will recover but by time."[13] Since it would have been highly unlikely for Humphries to have recovered from a stroke in time to fight another match with Mendoza the next year, and since no other newspaper reported what would have been a very serious development in the Mendoza-Humphries rivalry, I decided not to include a stroke in the graphic history.

In some cases, even corroboration did not guarantee that a claim was correct. For example, three newspapers, the *General Evening Post*, the *Gazetteer and New Daily Advertiser*, and the *London Chronicle*, used exactly the same wording to claim that during the second round of the Doncaster match Humphries "sprained his knee so violently, that it was supposed he could not stand up to continue the fight."[14] But the newspaper known as *Diary or Woodfall's Register* gave me what I considered good reasons to think that this claim, "which was circulated by some persons, and stated in several of yesterday's papers, was extremely fallacious as well as injudicious; for the second round was over in less than five minutes,

---

[13]*World*, Friday, May 8, 1789, Issue 734.

[14]*General Evening Post*, September 30, 1790–October 2, 1790; *Gazetteer and New Daily Advertiser*, Friday, October 1, 1790; and *London Chronicle*, September 30, 1790–October 2, 1790.

and Humphries fought an hour afterwards,— and that occasionally with great spirit—which would have been impossible had such an accident happened."[15] So I decided not to include a knee injury in the story.

TAKING LIBERTIES

Though I was careful to keep the story close to reliable sources, I nevertheless took liberties to conform to the art form of the graphic narrative. Comics usually have speech bubbles, and this meant creating dialogue, but the words of people in the past are much harder to come by than their actions. Even when famous speeches were recorded, they were taken down by secretaries who often made transcription errors. Ordinary conversation is for the most part lost to historians. In some cases it was possible to reconstruct dialogue on the basis of sources. For example, the heated conversation between Mendoza and Humphries in Chapter 4 is taken from newspaper accounts of July 7 and 8, 1788, though we can't be certain that the reporter transcribed the dialogue precisely.[16] Similarly, Mendoza's defense of boxing before Sir Sampson Wright at the Bow Street Court (depicted in Chapter 5) was related in numerous newspapers, though they did not report his exact words.

In other cases I put words in Mendoza's mouth that he expressed in written form elsewhere. For example, I don't know what Mendoza said to the audiences at his boxing academies (depicted in Chapter 2), but I do know what he wrote in his *Art of Boxing*, and it seemed plausible to me that he would have related the same ideas in his demonstrations. Similarly, I don't know the content of his conversations with Esther, but he reported in his memoirs how she felt about boxing, so I believe the dialogue I created between them was realistic. When justifying these decisions I take comfort in the words of the ancient Greek historian Thucydides, whose work included lengthy speeches that he himself had never heard: "my method has been, while keeping as closely as possible to the general sense of the words that were actually used, to make the speakers say what, in my opinion, was called for by each situation."[17] Not that I'm comparing

---

[15]*Diary or Woodfall's Register*, Saturday, October 2, 1790.

[16]*Morning Chronicle and London Advertiser*, Monday, July 7, 1788; *Public Advertiser*, Tuesday, July 8, 1788; and *World*, Tuesday, July 8, 1788. Mendoza reported the same conversation in his memoirs, but he was quoting the newspaper accounts. *Memoirs*, 112–21.

[17]Thucydides, *The Peloponnesian War*, translated by Rex Warner, with an introduction and notes by M. I. Finley (Harmondsworth, UK: Penguin, 1982), 47.

myself to Thucydides(!), but if this practice was good enough for him, it's good enough for me.

In some cases, however, for the sake of illustrating social types or simply for creating dramatic effect or comic relief, I invented characters as well as their speech. Thus the children waiting outside Mendoza's academy in Capel Court, the gentlemen standing in line outside the Panten Street academy, the women watching Mendoza demonstrate his art at the Lyceum Theatre, the father and son pair at the Doncaster match, and the men sitting on the park bench discussing Mendoza's death announcement are entirely imagined.

HISTORY AS A COLLABORATIVE ENTERPRISE

In addition to the sample chapter and the text for the rest of the graphic history, the proposal contained the primary sources you have read in Part II. It also included an outline of Part III (the essay on historical context) and Part IV (the account you are now reading), as well as the suggested written assignments in Part V. Once it was finished, Charles sent it to instructors at various colleges and universities for their feedback, and nine of them wrote reports assessing the project. The reports were sufficiently enthusiastic for Charles to present them to the editorial board, which approved the book for publication.

Over the course of the next four months Liz and I exchanged hundreds of emails. Liz asked me many questions that required me to go back through my notes or conduct new research. Some of these questions saved me from embarrassing errors. For example, some contemporary documents mentioned that Mendoza had an "academy" in Capel Court, and other documents indicated that he had one in Bartholomew Lane. I assumed that these were two different places, and that Mendoza had one academy at each address, and I claimed as much in my textual storyboard. But when Liz asked me whether the clientele at the two schools would have been similar or different, I looked in an eighteenth-century commercial directory to learn more about the neighborhoods and discovered that Capel Court was *in* Bartholomew Lane. There was only one academy in that neighborhood, and its address was "No. 4, Capel Court, Bartholomew Lane."

I continued to send Liz as many relevant images as I could find. Some of these I found in on the Internet, especially on museum websites and in image databases. Others could be found only in books, the old-fashioned kind made out of paper and found on library shelves. My university library was invaluable in helping me. I was a frequent patron of the inter-library loan department, and the highly talented reference librarian Kathleen

DeLaurenti helped me find images that I was having trouble finding on my own.

Charles played an active role in every aspect of this book's production, beginning by encouraging me and Liz to submit a proposal to Oxford University Press. He carefully read the graphic history and supplementary materials (including this essay) and made comments and suggestions in hundreds of emails. He provided ideas about the book's design, including the cover, endpapers (the leaves pasted to the cover at the front and back of the book), frontispiece (the first page), part openers (the three pages before each of the book's parts), and maps.

Reflecting on the process by which *Mendoza the Jew* came into being gives me a keen sense of the collaborative nature of my discipline. Historians often see their labor as solitary, in contrast to that of scientists or social scientists, who often work in groups. But my experience was far from solitary. Of course I worked most intensively with Liz, but many others made this book possible. I have mentioned Karlyn, Charles, Sagra, and Kathleen, and the instructors who provided feedback on the book proposal, though many more people at Oxford University Press have worked on the project in one capacity or another. Yet the book also drew on the work of people like Lewis Edwards and the many writers whose books and articles I cited in Part III. It depended on the work of those who compiled the massive databases I consulted when conducting research, not to mention the people who wrote those sources in the first place, from anonymous reporters to the story's principal characters: Humphries and Mendoza.

Let the collaboration continue. I don't want to have the last word on Mendoza. Just because a book has been produced doesn't mean the subject has been dealt with definitively. History is about interpretation. Now it's your turn.

PART V

NOW IT'S YOUR TURN

At this point you have read a graphic history, primary sources that served as the basis for it, an essay providing historical context, and an account of the making of *Mendoza the Jew*. By now you have a fairly good idea of what historians do. But you'll have an even better idea if you try it yourself. There's nothing mysterious or magical about what historians do: we read sources and interpret them. You can do it too. In this section you will see three types of suggested written assignments: short papers (roughly 500 to 1000 words), medium-length papers (roughly 1000 to 2000 words) and long papers (roughly 2000 to 4000 words). If you are reading this book for a course, your instructor might assign a paper from the topics suggested below. If you are reading it on your own, try a topic and paper length that appeal to you. In either case, before you know it you'll be your own historian.

Short Papers (suggested length: 500–1000 words)

1. Choose one of the letters that Mendoza or Humphries wrote to the editor of a newspaper in which the writer justified his behavior at a match, challenged his opponent to a rematch, and/or set conditions to the next fight. Briefly describe the content of the letter. Next discuss the claims the writer made. Which ones strike you as most believable, and why? Which claims are simply facts (which you may or may not be skeptical about), and which ones are value judgments? Finally, discuss some of the most important value judgments that are either explicitly stated or implicit (i.e., between the lines). In other words, discuss what the author of the letter considered morally right and wrong, or virtuous and unethical, and show how the author attributed positive characteristics to himself and negative characteristics to his opponent.

2. Choose a newspaper account of one of the three fights between Mendoza and Humphries. Briefly relate the narrative or story. (Don't feel compelled to include all the details, especially if the article is long.) Which of the claims strike you as most believable, and which ones are you more skeptical about? (Explain your reasoning.) Which of the claims

are simply facts (which you may choose to doubt), and which ones are value judgments? In addition, discuss some of the most important value judgments, keeping in mind that some are explicitly stated and others are implicitly conveyed (i.e., between the lines). In other words, discuss what the author of the letter considered morally right and wrong, or virtuous and unethical. In addition, does the article try to persuade you that one of the fighters behaved better than the other? If so, to what extent are you convinced by the article's judgment of the fighters? (Again, explain your reasoning.) Is the article biased or fair?

3. Read one of the pre-fight agreements between Mendoza and Humphries. Restate the conditions in everyday language. (You may find the glossary at the end of this book helpful.) To what degree does the agreement reveal the suspicion the two fighters had of each other? What improper behavior did they anticipate? What does the agreement reveal about the moral qualities the boxers valued? Which qualities did they consider virtuous, and which ones did they consider unethical? Finally, can you derive any clues from the agreement regarding the values of British people more generally at the time the agreement was written? If so, what does the document tell us about what those values were?

4. Closely examine one of the Gillray prints reproduced in Part II. Describe what you see, relating the most noticeable features of the picture. (Don't feel compelled to write down everything you see.) Also summarize the caption, highlighting the main idea Gillray wanted to convey about the match. Which moment in the fight did he capture, and why? How did the specific event in the match highlight Gillray's message? And what was that message? Who, according to Gillray, was the more praiseworthy boxer, and how did he convey his opinion? (Consider both the picture and the caption.)

Medium-Length Papers (suggested length: 1000–2000 words)

1. Choose one of the three matches—Odiham, Stilton, or Doncaster—and read the newspaper stories about them. Using these various accounts, provide a narrative of the match. Cite the documents for each of your claims, noting where more than one newspaper reported the same thing. Then discuss the main controversy or controversies in the match and how the newspapers reported on it/them. Did one or more newspapers have a favorite? If so, how did it/they express this favoritism? Did anti-Semitism (anti-Jewish prejudice) play a role in any of the reporting? If

so, explain how. Finally, which of the newspapers' claims seem most believable to you, and why? Which ones seem least believable, and why?

2. Choose one of the three matches—Odiham, Stilton, or Doncaster—and compare Mendoza's memoir account to those of the newspapers. (Do not use his letters to the editor for this assignment.) Where does Mendoza's account corroborate/confirm those of the newspapers? Where does his account differ from those of the newspapers? In the cases of divergence, what accounts for these differences? To what extent is Mendoza's account self-serving? In other words, to what extent did Mendoza choose or interpret events to make himself look good? (Give examples from the text.) To what extent and in which cases do you think faulty memory accounts for the discrepancies? (Mendoza wrote his memoirs approximately 20 years after the matches he described.) Finally, do you think memoirs are more problematic (subject to skepticism) than newspaper accounts? Why or why not?

3. Analyze the correspondence between Mendoza and Humphries. On the basis of their letters, what do you infer their values to be? What characteristics do the two boxers consider virtuous, and which ones do they disdain? How does each boxer try to make himself look good and the other bad? How honest or accurate is each one in his claims? What do you think the correspondence might say about British values of the time?

4. Examine the three Gillray prints. Describe the information they contain about the fights. (Consider both the pictures and the captions.) But also show how the prints do more than simply relate information. Show how they convey Gillray's point/s of view. How did Gillray view Mendoza and Humphries? Did he believe that one of them behaved more honorably or virtuously than the other? Did his opinion change on the basis of the match he was depicting? Choosing selectively from the other sources, discuss how reliable you think Gillray's prints were.

5. The *Whitehall Evening Post* and the *World* newspapers covered all three of the Mendoza-Humphries matches, and their reports are in Part II of this book. Discuss the two newspapers' coverage of the rivalry. Did the newspapers have an editorial bias—in other words, did they favor one contestant over the other? If so, which paper was more favorable to Mendoza, and which to Humphries? Did the newspapers change their opinion of one or both of the boxers over time? Apart from the course of the matches, what else did the newspapers tend to notice? Does one

newspaper seem more reliable to you than the other as a historical source? Why or why not?

Long Papers (suggested length: 2000–4000 words)

1. By the time of the Doncaster fight, the newspapers (and Gillray) seem to have shown more respect for Mendoza than they did at the time of the Odiham fight. Did these commentators change their attitude over the course of the nearly three-year period, or did Mendoza change his behavior in that time? Whatever your answer is (including "both"), be sure to explain your reasoning.

2. Using the sources in Part II of this book, comment on the following claim: The Mendoza-Humphries rivalry is a window onto British society at the time; the competition and its coverage in the newspapers and in Gillray prints reveal much about the ideas, practices, and interests of the British public.

3. Choose a specific theme (such as gender, class relations, health, leisure, gambling, tolerance, anti-Semitism) and discuss what the Mendoza-Humphries rivalry tells us about this theme in late eighteenth-century Britain.

4. Using the sources in Part II, assess the account of the three Mendoza-Humphries matches as they are depicted in Part I (the graphic history). To what extent did the author and artist provide an accurate and thorough account of the matches? Did they depict one of the fighters more sympathetically or more generously than they depicted the other? If so, was this justified? What did you learn from the primary sources that the graphic history didn't mention? Were these omissions from the graphic history justified? Insofar as the primary sources frequently offered conflicting views of the matches, which of these views did the author and artist present, and which ones did they seem to discount? If you had the opportunity to write a history (graphic or otherwise) of the Mendoza-Humphries rivalry, what would you have emphasized, and what would you have downplayed? What other strengths and weaknesses in the graphic history do the primary sources reveal?

5. You have examined three types of sources: a memoir, newspapers, and prints. What are the strengths and weaknesses of these kinds of sources for historical study? Be sure to cite specific sources when supporting your claims.

BIBLIOGRAPHY

PRIMARY SOURCES

NEWSPAPERS

Argus
Bath Chronicle
Bristol Mercury
Bury and Norwich Post
Calcutta Chronicle and General
  Advertiser
Caledonian Mercury
Champion and Weekly Herald
Courier and Evening Gazette
Diary or Woodfall's Register
Derby Mercury
E. Johnson's British Gazette and
  Sunday Monitor
English Chronicle or Universal
  Evening Post
Era
Examiner
Felix Farley's Bristol Journal
Gazetteer and New Daily
  Advertiser
General Evening Post
Glasgow Herald
Hampshire Telegraph and Sussex
  Chronicle
Hull Packet and Humber
  Mercury
India Gazette
Ipswich Journal
Jackson's Oxford Journal
Lancaster Gazette and General
  Advertiser

Leeds Mercury
Lloyd's Evening Post
London Chronicle
London Evening Post
London Packet or New Lloyd's
  Evening Post
Morning Chronicle and London
  Advertiser
Morning Herald
Morning Post
Morning Post and Daily
  Advertiser
Morning Post and Fashionable
  World
Morning Post and Gazetteer
Morning Star
Oracle
Oracle and Daily Advertiser
Oracle and Public Advertiser
Oracle Bell's New World
Public Advertiser
Royal Cornwall Gazette, Fal-
  mouth Packet & Plymouth
  Journal
St. James's Chronicle or the Brit-
  ish Evening Post
Star
Sun
Sunday Reformer and Universal
  Register
Times

Trewman's Exeter Flying Post or Plymouth and Cornish Advertiser

Whitehall Evening Post

World

World and Fashionable Advertiser

York Herald

BOOKS AND ARTICLES

Adeline; or the Orphan. London, 1790.

Andrews, Miles Peter. "The Muses in Motion, Spoken at the Royalty Theatre, by Mrs. Hudson and Mrs. Gibbs. In the Characters of the Tragic and Comic Muse," in *The European Magazine, and London Review; Containing the Literature, History, Politics, Arts, Manners and Amusements of the Age. . . .* London, 1788. Vol. 13, pp. 56–57.

Barnett, Lionel D., et al. *Bevis Marks Records: Being Contributions to the History of the Spanish and Portuguese Congregation of London*. Oxford: Oxford University Press, 1940. 6 vols.

Broughton, John. *Proposals for Erecting an Amphitheatre for the Manly Exercise of Boxing, by John Broughton, Professor of Athletics*. [London, 1743].

Egan, Pierce. *Boxiana; Or, Sketches of Ancient and Modern Pugilism*. London, 1812; reprint, 1830. Vol. 1.

"Epistle from Quondam in the Country, to his Cousin Quoz. By an Oxford Correspondent," *The Attic Miscellany; and Characteristic Mirror of Men and Things. Including the Correspondent's Museum. Volume the First*. London, 1791. Vol. 1, pp. 153–55.

Joanides, Alex, ed. *Memoirs of the Life of Daniel Mendoza (1816)*. London: Romewille Enterprises, 2011.

Lemoine, Henry. *Modern Manhood; or, The Art and Practice of English Boxing. Including the History of the Science of Natural Self-Defence; and Memoirs of the Most Celebrated Practitioners of that Manly Exercise*. London, [1788?].

Mendoza, Daniel. *The Art of Boxing: With a Statement of the Transactions that Have Passed between Mr. Humphreys and Myself Since our Battle at Odiham*. London, 1789.

Mendoza, Daniel. *Memoirs of the Life of Daniel Mendoza; Containing a Faithful Narrative of the Various Vicissitudes of his Life, and an Account of the Numerous Contests in which he has been Engaged, with Observations on Each; Comprising also Genuine Anecdotes of Many Distinguished Characters, to which are Added, Observations on the Art of Pugilism; Rules to be Observed with Regard to Training, &c*. London, 1816.

The Odiad; or, Battle of Humphries and Mendoza; An Heroic Poem. Humbly Dedicated to the Two Boxing Academies. Several Illustriaous Personages, the Patrons and Amateurs of this Most Anciennt Art, are Justly Celebrated in the Work. To this is Added, A Prefatory Dissertation on Boxing, in Which Some Ingenious Observations on its Utility are Most Seriously Submitted to the Consideration of the Legislature. London, 1788.

Pancratia, or A History of Pugilism. Containing a Full Account of Every Battle of Note from the Time of Broughton and Slack, down to the Present Day. Interspersed with Anecdotes of all the Celebrated Pugilists of this Country; With an Argumentative Proof, that Pugilism, Considered as a Gymnic Exercise, Demands the Admiration, and Patronage of Every Free State, Being Calculated to Inspire Manly Courage, and a Spirit of Independence—Enabling Us to Resist Slavery at Home and Enemies from Abroad. Embellished with a Correct and Elegant Engraved Portrait of the Champion, Crib. London, 1812.

SECONDARY

Bell, David A. *The Cult of the Nation in France: Inventing Nationalism, 1680–1800*. Cambridge, MA: Harvard University Press, 2001.

Berkowitz, Michael, and Ruti Ungar, eds. *Fighting Back? Jewish and Black Boxers in Britain*. London: University College London, 2007.

Brailsford, Dennis. *Bareknuckles: A Social History of Prize-Fighting*. Cambridge, UK: Lutterworth Press, 1988.

Brailsford, Dennis. *A Taste for Diversions: Sport in Georgian England*. Cambridge, UK: Lutterworth Press, 1999.

Briggs, Peter, M. "Daniel Mendoza and Sporting Celebrity: A Case Study." In *Romanticism and Celebrity Culture, 1750–1850*, edited by Tom Mole, 103–19. Cambridge: Cambridge University Press, 2009.

Colley, Linda. *Britons: Forging the Nation, 1707–1837*. New Haven, CT: Yale University Press, 1992.

Cunningham, Hugh. *Leisure in the Industrial Revolution*. London: Croom Helm, 1980.

Edwards, Lewis. "Daniel Mendoza." In *The Jewish Historical Society of England. Transactions: Sessions 1939–1945*. London: Edward Goldston, 1946. Vol. 15, pp. 73–92.

Endelman, Todd M. *The Jews of Britain, 1656 to 2000*. Berkeley: University of California Press, 2002.

Endelman, Todd M. *The Jews of Georgian England, 1714–1837: Tradition and Change in a Liberal Society*. Philadelphia: Jewish Publication Society of America, 1979.

Endelman, Todd M. *Radical Assimilation in English Jewish History: 1656–1945*. Bloomington: Indiana University Press, 1990.

Ford, John. *Prizefighting: The Age of Regency Boximania*. Newton Abbot, UK: David and Charles, 1971.

Gee, Tony. *Up to Scratch: Bareknuckle Fighting and Heroes of the Prize-Ring*. Harpenden, Herts, UK: Queen Anne Press, 1998.

Huizinga, Johan. *Homo Ludens: A Study of the Play Element in Culture*. Boston: Beacon Press, 1955.

Johnson, Christopher. "' British Championism': Early Pugilism and the Works of Fielding." *Review of English Studies* 47 (August 1996): 331–51.

Katz, David. *Philo-Semitism and the Readmission of the Jews to England, 1603–1655*. Oxford, UK: Clarendon Press, 1982.

Katz, David. *Jews in the History of England, 1485–1850*. Oxford: Oxford University Press, 1994.

Kent, Susan Kingsley. *Gender and Power in Britain, 1640–1990*. London and New York: Routledge, 1999.

Mee, Bob. *Bare Fists: The History of Bare-Knuckle Prize-Fighting*. Woodstock, NY: Overlook Press, 2001.

Olsen, Kirstin. *Daily Life in 18th-Century England*. Westport, CT: Greenwood Press, 1999.

Plumb, J[ohn] H[arold]. *The Commercialisation of Leisure in Eighteenth-Century England*. Reading, UK: Reading University, 1973.

Pollins, Harold. *Economic History of the Jews in England*. London and Toronto: Associated University Presses, 1982.

Ribalow, Harold U. *Fighter from Whitechapel: The Story of Daniel Mendoza*. New York: Farrar, Straus and Cudahy, 1962. Illustrated by Simon Jeruchim.

Roth, Cecil. *A History of the Jews in England*. Oxford: Oxford University Press, 1941; reprint, 1964.

Scott, Joan. "Gender: A Useful Category of Historical Analysis." *The American Historical Review* 91 (December 1986): 1053–1075.

Schama, Simon. "The King's Pugilist: Daniel Mendoza (1764–1836)." In *Jewish Jocks: An Unorthodox Hall of Fame,* edited by Franklin Foer and Marc Tracy, 2–12. New York and Boston: Twelve, 2012.

Tranter, Neil. *Sport, Economy and Society in Britain, 1750–1914.* Cambridge: Cambridge University Press, 1998.

Ungar, Ruti. "The Boxing Discourse in Late Georgian England, 1780–1820: A Study in Civic Humanism, Gender, Class and Race." PhD diss., Humboldt University of Berlin, 2010.

Warhman, Dror. *The Making of the Modern Self: Identity and Culture in Eighteenth-Century England.* New Haven, CT: Yale University Press, 2004.

Whale, John. "Daniel Mendoza's Contests of Identity: Masculinity, Ethnicity and Nation in Georgian Prize-Fighting." *Romanticism* 14 (October 2008): 259–71.

White, Jerry. *London in the Eighteenth Century: A Great and Monstrous Thing.* London: Bodley Head, 2012.

GLOSSARY

AMATEUR: literally a lover, figuratively an enthusiast of something (for example, a sport); amateurs of boxing did not themselves necessarily box.

ARTICLES OF AGREEMENT: the contract between the boxers laying out the rules by which a match is to be fought.

BOTTLE-HOLDER: the person who waits on a boxer during a match, providing water and other necessities.

BOTTOM: ability and willingness to persevere.

BYE-BATTLE: an impromptu secondary fight, usually following the main event.

CANT: to turn (something or someone) upside down.

CLOSE: to hold the opponent in a kind of forced hug (a tactic now known as "clinching"); a means of shortening the distance, and hence the force, of the opponent's punches.

COUP DE MAIN: a sudden and powerful attack.

CROSS: a fixed match; to "fight a cross" was to lose deliberately in order to receive payment from gamblers who bet on the other contestant.

CROSS-BUTTOCK: a wrestling move in which one's hip is used as leverage in "throwing" an opponent.

DEPOSIT: the money raised by a boxer for his share of the stakes and left with a stake-holder until the end of the match.

DOOR-MONEY: the money collected from ticket purchasers; sometimes shortened to "the door."

DRESS: to beat thoroughly, to thrash.

DROP: to fall deliberately, without being forced to the ground by a blow. See "shift."

DUKE'S PLACE: a square in East London in the heart of the Jewish neighborhood. The term also refers figuratively to the Jewish community.

FEINT: a false attack; a blow seemingly directed at one body part while the real object of attack is elsewhere.

GAME: as an adjective it means spirited or courageous; as a noun it indicates fighting spirit or strong character.

GATE MONEY: see "door-money."

GUARD: a defensive stance.

GUINEA: a gold coin worth 5 percent more than a pound.

KNOWING ONES: self-proclaimed experts, people with reputed knowledge, especially of a sport.

LOINS: area on both sides of the backbone between the lower ribs and the hips. Loin pain is sometimes a sign of kidney trouble.

LOVE: pleasure (of engaging in the sport); to fight "for love" was to fight without any prize money at stake.

NEAT: skillful, well-executed.

ONSET: attack or onslaught.

PARRY: to block or stop (a punch); also figuratively, to avert or avoid something unpleasant.

ROUND BLOW: a hook punch (as in "a left hook").

SCIENCE: skill that comes as the result of methodical training.

SCREW: to twist one's knuckles into an opponent, especially his nose or eye.

SECOND: a kind of coach who could also intervene in a fight to block an unfair blow.

SET-TO (OR "SETT-TO"): to begin fighting, or (as a noun) the beginning of a fight or round.

SHIFT: to fall deliberately to the platform or ground; a means of ending the round and generally considered "unmanly" and unfair. See also "drop."

SMART: energetic or quick; hard enough to cause pain (as in a blow).

SOMERSET: somersault.

STAKE-HOLDER: the person entrusted with the prize money.

STOP: to block or parry (a punch).

STRIP: to remove one's ordinary clothing; in the context of a boxing match it does *not* mean to remove all of one's clothing. Boxers stripped to the waist, removing their coats, vests, and shirts.

THROW: to push (an opponent) to the ground.

WIND: capacity to breathe. A boxer with "wind" was in good physical (especially aerobic) shape.